PRESIDENTS
and their
DECISIONS

ABRAHAM
LINCOLN

HELEN COTHRAN, *Book Editor*

BONNIE SZUMSKI, *Editorial Director*
SCOTT BARBOUR, *Managing Editor*
JAMES D. TORR, *Series Editor*

GREENHAVEN PRESS, INC.
SAN DIEGO, CALIFORNIA

Every effort has been made to trace the owners of copyrighted material. The articles in this volume may have been edited for content,
length, and/or reading level. The titles have been changed to enhance
the editorial purpose.

No part of this book may be reproduced or used in any form or by any
means, electrical, mechanical, or otherwise, including, but not limited
to, photocopy, recording, or any information storage and retrieval system without prior written permission from the publisher.

Library of Congress Cataloging-in-Publication Data

Abraham Lincoln / Helen Cothran, book editor.
    p. cm. — (Presidents and their decisions)
    Includes bibliographical references and index.
    ISBN 0-7377-0917-0 (lib. bdg. : alk. paper) — ISBN 0-7377-0916-2
(pbk. : alk. paper)
    1. Lincoln, Abraham, 1809–1865. 2. United States—Politics and gov-
ernment—1861–1865—Decision making. I. Cothran, Helen. II. Series.

E456 .A28 2002
973.7'902—dc21   2001023831
                                                            CIP

Cover photo: Library of Congress

Series Design: LiMiTeD Edition Book Design, Linda Mae Tratechaud

© 2002 Greenhaven Press, Inc.
P.O. Box 289009, San Diego, CA 92198-9009

PRINTED IN THE U.S.A.

CONTENTS

Foreword   7

Abraham Lincoln: A Biography   10

CHAPTER 1: THE OUTBREAK OF CIVIL WAR

1. Averting Civil War: Lincoln Should Have Supported
   the Crittenden Compromise *by David M. Potter*   32

   Lincoln should have supported the Crittenden Compromise, which included provisions regarding slavery that
   would have appeased both Southern secessionists and
   Northern abolitionists. Without support from Lincoln,
   the plan failed to pass in the Senate and all hope of keeping compromise alive and averting civil war perished.

2. Lincoln's Handling of the Political Battle That Led
   to the Civil War *by Frank van der Linden*   39

   Lincoln was pressured by several opposing political
   groups during the secession crisis of 1861. In the end, the
   president sided with radical Republicans who advocated
   the use of force against the South, thus putting partisan
   politics above the lives of thousands.

3. The Crisis at Fort Sumter: Lincoln Provoked the
   South into War *by John Shipley Tilley*   51

   Lincoln sent an expedition to provision Fort Sumter to
   deliberately provoke the Confederacy into trying to stop
   the plan. Lincoln knew that his scheme would force the
   South to fire the first shot of civil war and would garner
   public support for his goal of forcing the seceding states
   back into the Union.

4. Lincoln Did Not Deliberately Provoke War at
   Fort Sumter *by Richard N. Current*   57

   Lincoln believed that it was possible for the Union to
   provision Fort Sumter without provoking the Confederate army to fire on the fort. However, if a first shot was

fired, Lincoln wanted the aggression to come from the Confederates so that public opinion would turn against the South.

5. Lincoln's Commitment to Saving the Union
   by Lord Charnwood   63

   If the Southern states were allowed to secede, it would
   have destroyed the political integrity of the United States.
   Lincoln was justified in attempting to preserve the
   world's first experiment in democracy.

6. How Lincoln Justified the War: From
   Preserving the Union to Abolishing Slavery
   by Kenneth M. Stampp   73

   When the Southern states seceded, Lincoln initially justified war on the grounds that the Union must be saved.
   However, Lincoln eventually came to feel that saving the
   Union was an inadequate moral justification for such a
   long and bloody war and instead adopted the cause of
   emancipation.

CHAPTER 2: SUSPENSION OF THE WRIT OF HABEAS CORPUS

1. Lincoln's Temporary Dictatorship
   by William Archibald Dunning   84

   Lincoln established a temporary dictatorship when he suspended the writ of habeas corpus in 1861. Although his
   decision led to the repression of civil liberties as outlined
   in the Constitution, it ultimately helped save the Union.

2. Lincoln Was Right to Suspend the Writ of Habeas
   Corpus *by J.G. Randall*   90

   The secession crisis of 1861constituted a rebellion, and
   the Constitution allows for suspension of the writ in
   such emergencies.

3. Lincoln Reluctantly Carried Out a Policy of
   Repression *by Dean Sprague*   98

   Lincoln suspended the writ of habeas corpus reluctantly
   and mitigated the suspension's effects as best he could by
   treating prisoners humanely.

4. Lincoln's Repression of Civil Liberties Has Been
Exaggerated *by James M. McPherson*   104
Critics have unfairly blamed Lincoln for carrying out a
policy of repression. Suspension of the writ of habeas corpus was necessary to stop anti-Union activities, and the
repression of civil liberties that resulted was not excessive.

CHAPTER 3: THE GREAT EMANCIPATOR

1. The Emancipation Proclamation Freed the Slaves
by John Hope Franklin   111
When Lincoln issued the Emancipation Proclamation, he
transformed the war from a fight to save the Union to a
higher moral battle to emancipate the slaves. The Proclamation demoralized the South and fortified the North,
which made Union victory—and with it, total emancipation—possible.

2. Radical Republicans in Congress Forced Lincoln
to Adopt Emancipation *by T. Harry Williams*   119
Lincoln was forced by the anti-slavery radicals to issue
the Emancipation Proclamation. The president preferred
the more conservative route of compensated emancipation over time, but he knew that he needed the radicals'
support in order to win the war and save the Union.

3. Lincoln Held a Lifelong Commitment to
Emancipation *by LaWanda Cox*   129
Lincoln deserves the title of "The Great Emancipator."
Although he frequently had to steer a middle course to
appease conservatives, Lincoln nevertheless worked con-
sistently toward emancipation.

4. Lincoln Believed That Saving the Union and
Ending Slavery Were Inseparable Goals
by David Livingstone   138
Lincoln believed that slavery itself threatened the Union,
since it contradicted the tenet that all men are created
equal. Therefore, Lincoln viewed emancipation and the
preservation of the Union as inseparable goals.

CHAPTER 4: RECONSTRUCTION

1. The Price of Conservatism: The Failure of
   Lincoln's 10 Percent Plan *by Avery Craven*   146

   Lincoln's plan for Reconstruction was too conservative to
   have achieved the racial equality that was necessary for
   the security of freed slaves. Moreover, it failed to enforce
   social integration of the freedmen or to alter Southern
   attitudes on class.

2. Lincoln's Reconstruction Plan Became
   Increasingly Radical by *Hans L. Trefousse*   154

   Over time Lincoln altered his ideas on Reconstruction to
   accommodate the radical Republicans' plans, which
   promised to offer freed slaves more equality than his successor, Andrew Johnson, eventually secured for them
   after Lincoln's death.

3. All of Lincoln's Reconstruction Plans Failed
   by William B. Hesseltine   167

   Every one of Lincoln's plans for Reconstruction failed
   because he conceded to conservative and radical pressure. At the time of his assassination, he had no plan to
   reintroduce the seceded states back into the Union.

4. Lincoln Was Responsible for the Passage of
   the Thirteenth Amendment
   by J.G. Randall and Richard N. Current   178

   Lincoln succeeded in getting the Thirty-Eighth Congress
   to pass the Thirteenth Amendment abolishing slavery.
   Through Lincoln's influence, enough Democrats changed
   their votes to enable the Amendment to pass at least a
   year sooner than it otherwise would have.

Appendix of Documents   190
Chronology   211
For Further Research   216
Index   219

FOREWORD

66"T HE PRESIDENCY OF THE UNITED STATES IS OFTEN DE-
scribed as the most powerful office in the world,"
writes Forrest McDonald in *The American Presidency: An
Intellectual History*. "In one sense this description is accurate," he says, "for even casual decisions made in the White
House can affect the lives of millions of people." But Mc-
Donald also notes that presidential power "is restrained by
the countervailing power of Congress, the courts, the bu-
reaucracy, popular opinion, the news media, and state and
local governments. What presidents do have is awesome
responsibilities combined with unique opportunities to
persuade others to do their bidding—opportunities en-
hanced by the possibility of dispensing favors, by the mys-
tique of presidential power, and by the aura of monarchy
that surrounds the president."

The way various presidents have used the complex
power of their office is the subject of Greenhaven Press's
Presidents and Their Decisions series. Each volume in the
series examines one particular president and the key decisions he made while in office.

Some presidential decisions have been made in a relatively brief period of time, as with Abraham Lincoln's suspension of the writ of habeus corpus at the start of the
Civil War. Others were refined as they were implemented
over a period of years, as was the case with Franklin De-
lano Roosevelt's struggle to lead the country out of the
Great Depression. Some presidential actions are generally
lauded by historians—for example, Lyndon Johnson's support of the civil rights movement in the 1960s—while others have been condemned—such as Richard Nixon's ef-

forts, from 1972 to 1974, to cover up the involvement of his aides in the Watergate scandal.

Most of the truly history-making presidential decisions, though, remain the subject of intense scrutiny and historical debate. Many of these were made during a time of war or other crisis, in which a president was forced to risk either spectacular success or devastating failure. Examples include Lincoln's much-scrutinized handling of the crisis at Fort Sumter, the first conflict of the Civil War; FDR's efforts to aid the European Allies at the beginning of World War II; Harry Truman's controversial decision to use the atomic bomb in order to end that conflict; and Lyndon Johnson's fateful decision to escalate the war in Vietnam.

Each volume in the Presidents and Their Decisions series devotes a full chapter to each of the president's key decisions. The essays in each chapter, most written by presidential historians and biographers, offer a range of perspectives on the president and his actions. Some provide background on the political, social, and economic factors behind a particular decision. Others critique the president's performance, offering a negative or positive appraisal. Essays have been chosen for their concise and engaging presentation of the facts, and each is preceded by a straightforward summary of the article's content.

In addition to the articles, these books include extensive material to help the student researcher. An opening essay provides both a brief biography of the president and an overview of the events that occurred during his time in office. A chronology also helps readers keep track of the dates of specific events. A comprehensive index and an annotated table of contents aid readers in quickly locating material of interest, and an extensive bibliography serves as a launching point for further research. Finally, an appendix of primary historical documents provides a sampling of the president's most important speeches, as well as some of his contemporaries' criticisms.

Greenhaven Press's Presidents and Their Decisions series will help students gain a deeper understanding of the decisions made by some of the most influential leaders in American history.

F OR WEEKS THE DEAD LAY ON THE BATTLEFIELD AT GETTYS-burg, grim testimony to the bloodiest and most decisive battle during the Civil War. To honor the thousands who had died in the battle, a great national cemetery was proposed on the Gettysburg site. On November 19, 1863, the president of the United States stepped before a crowd that had assembled to dedicate the cemetery. Abraham Lincoln delivered his ten-sentence Gettysburg address in mere minutes, reminding the nation of why the war was being fought. He asked that the American people resolve "that these dead shall not have died in vain—that this nation, under God, shall have a new birth of freedom—and that government of the people, by the people, for the people, shall not perish from the earth."[1]

In Lincoln's address, he articulated the reason why he was willing to lead his country into what would turn out to be America's most costly war. The Declaration of Independence, he argued, had set down the principles of freedom, equality and democracy upon which the nation had been founded. That document had then become the basis for the U.S. Constitution, which as president he had sworn to uphold. The war, Lincoln said, was being fought to honor the sentiments behind the documents, to save the Union and preserve the world's first experiment in democracy.

These two documents shaped Lincoln's political life, and, somewhat ironically, generated much of the conflict he faced politically, especially throughout the war. On the one hand, the Declaration of Independence states that all men are created equal, which Lincoln interpreted to include slaves. On the other hand, the Constitution did not forbid slavery, nor did it implicitly give Congress or the president the authority to abolish it. Furthermore, the Constitution stresses the rights of the states to manage their own affairs and limits the power of the federal government. Lincoln's respect for both documents informed all of his political decisions, but he found himself struggling to act within the confines of the Constitution while still honoring the spirit of the Declaration. Of course, Lincoln was not the only one who used the documents to judge political actions—critics and supporters alike referred to them when castigating or praising Lincoln, which they did relentlessly throughout his political career.

During Lincoln's rise to national prominence, the country was in turmoil over slavery and the threat that some of the Southern states wanted to secede from the Union. In consequence, Lincoln followed a moderate course in order to win the most friends and gain the fewest enemies. Attacked on all sides, and constantly struggling to act in accordance with the nation's most important documents, Lincoln kept to the middle ground as much as was possible. The responsibility of a nation was riding on this man of humble beginnings.

Life on the Prairie

Abraham Lincoln was born on February 12, 1809, in a one-room log cabin on a farm near Hodgenville, Kentucky. Lincoln's father, Thomas, and his mother, Nancy, enjoyed the picturesque surroundings near their Kentucky farm, but the soil was rocky, making it difficult to farm. An ambitious man, Thomas decided to move the family when Lincoln was three years old to another Kentucky farm where the soil was more promising. Life on the prairie was still difficult, however, and Lincoln sometimes worked at the farm even after nightfall. As he began to develop a love for education, the young Lincoln grew increasingly frustrated with the lack of intellectual life on the prairie. In total, Lincoln received only about one year of formal education. Over the years, he developed his mind on his own, reading voraciously from favorite books such as a collection of Shakespeare's plays and the ancient Greek Euclid's text on geometry. The boy had inherited his father's ambition, but in the younger Lincoln it was to take a decidedly different direction.

The Lincolns' Kentucky farm was taken away from them in 1816 when Lincoln was seven because they did not have their ownership papers in order, and the family was forced to move again. As more and more poor white laborers were kicked off their land, more affluent landowners took over the farms and used their slaves to work them. As a young boy, Lincoln saw that slaves were forced to labor for nothing, which he felt was horrible enough, but he also saw that it was hard on poor white men who could not compete with them for work. It was clear to Lincoln that slavery removed all incentive to do good work and move up in the world for white and black alike. This early observation became the root of Lincoln's growing hatred of slavery.

In 1816, Thomas and Nancy moved to the Indiana Territory, where slavery was outlawed. Lincoln was only nine when his mother died, and a few years later his father married a widow name Sarah Bush Johnston, whom Lincoln grew to love intensely. For many of the years of his youth, Lincoln helped clear the forest of trees to make way for the farm and he grew strong and healthy. However, Lincoln always regretted this solitary labor because it kept him away from his books. While still a young man, Lincoln was criticized for being "lazy" because he would be seen in the middle of the day resting under a tree rather than wielding an axe. However, the young man was not lazing about—he was reading and trying to improve his mind. In 1830, the Lincoln family moved again, this time to Illinois.

A New Life in Politics

Tired of the drudgery of farm work, the eager young Lincoln began to travel. Eventually he settled down to work as a manager of a general store in New Salem, Illinois. As the store began doing less and less business and the town began to dwindle, Lincoln decided that he could do something to help. In 1832 at the age of twenty-three, he declared himself a candidate for the Illinois House of Representatives. Lincoln ran on an "internal improvements" platform, stating his intention to instigate large public works projects to improve the state's infrastructure. In particular, he wanted to improve the little Sangamon River—the lifeblood of New Salem—to make transportation on it easier. He also argued for more and better public schools, contending that every man should receive an education.

Unfortunately, Lincoln lost the election, but due to his increasing political reputation, was appointed as postmaster in 1833. A year later, in 1834, he again ran for the state legislature. This time, because he had become better known outside of New Salem, Lincoln won the seat. While working in the Illinois legislature, Lincoln began to study law at the suggestion of Whig Party originator John Todd Stuart, who was impressed with Lincoln's abilities. Lincoln was admitted to the bar in 1837 and eventually opened a law office in Springfield with Stuart.

Lincoln built his early political career as an industrialist, arguing for the development of railroads, banks, and canals as a way to alleviate the kind of poverty he had suffered as a child. Re-elected to the state assembly in 1836, 1838, and 1840 and gaining in reputation, Lincoln continued with his law studies when the legislature was not in session. During these later years of his service to the Illinois House of Representatives, the issue of slavery began to surface as a serious state and national issue, and Lincoln became an anti-slavery man as well as an industrialist. As abolitionism began to increase throughout the North, a resolution condemning abolitionists was presented to the Illinois General Assembly. Lincoln refused to sign the document, arguing that slavery was wrong. Lincoln's views against slavery were not shared by a majority of the people of Illinois, however, most of whom sympathized with Southern slaveholders.

Lincoln began to work for the burgeoning Whig Party, which he believed had the best chance of abolishing slavery, but he also continued to focus on his "internal improvements" plan. On May 2, 1846, the Whig Party named Lincoln as the Whig candidate for the U.S. House of Representatives, and he eventually beat Peter Cartwright to win the seat. As a congressional representative, Lincoln showed his concern for slavery early by introducing a bill that would free all children born to slaves in Washington, D.C. The measure was unsuccessful. When his congressional term was up in 1848, Lincoln returned to Springfield to devote himself to his family and to his law practice.

Lincoln had married Mary Todd of Lexington, Kentucky, in 1842, and together they had four sons, Robert, Edward, William, and Thomas. Many of those close to the Lincoln family thought Mary was materialistic and complaining, and the boys spoiled and undisciplined. However, Lincoln did not seem to mind his family's foibles, and apparently enjoyed spending time at home. For several years Lincoln was content to practice law in Springfield and be with his family, but in 1854, he was once again drawn into politics.

Road to the Presidency

An explosive piece of legislation was introduced to Congress by Illinois senator Stephen Douglas and passed in 1854. The Kansas-Nebraska Act allowed for the expansion of slavery into the territories, which in essence overturned the Missouri Compromise of 1820. The Missouri Compromise had made slavery legal south of the 36 degree latitude and illegal north of it. The Kansas-Nebraska Act allowed each new territory to decide for itself if it wanted to be slave or free, a process Douglas called "popular sovereignty." Lincoln detested the act, arguing that it promised to spread slavery, and he returned to politics in order to have a voice in the way the country was handling the slavery issue.

Lincoln's basic view on slavery was that it undermined a nation founded on liberty. But Lincoln was careful not to preach to the South on moral grounds because he thought such a stance would only create more division within the country. Instead, he argued against slavery in economic terms. He was an advocate of the "free labor system," which, he explained, "opens the way for all—gives hope to all, and energy, and progress, and improvement of condition to all."[2] He argued that because their slaves were unable to better their condition through their labor, the South had ceased to progress. In addition, he claimed that slavery degraded the dignity of all manual work and therefore demeaned white labor as well.

Lincoln's stance on slavery was challenged during his bid for the U.S. Senate in 1858. Lincoln had left the failing Whig Party and joined the growing Republican Party and was running on the Republican ticket. One of the great motivators for Lincoln's decision to run for a Senate seat was the Dred Scott case. In 1857, Supreme Court justice Roger B. Taney, who was sympathetic to Southern slave owners, had issued the famous decision. Scott, a slave, had sued for his freedom, but Taney declared that African-Americans were not citizens of the United States and therefore Scott could not sue in federal court. The Court also ruled that Congress could not prohibit slavery in the new territories. On June 16, 1858, Lincoln delivered his famous House Divided speech—which presaged the Civil War—in which he predicted that "this government cannot endure, permanently half *slave* and half *free* . . . It will become *all* one thing or *all* the other."[3] His Democratic opponent, Stephen Douglas, accused Lincoln of viewing African-Americans as equals to whites, hoping to incite the South and moderate Northerners to vote against Lincoln.

In response to Douglas's accusations, Lincoln proposed a series of seven debates, which would be carried out in various parts of Illinois. During these debates, which lasted from August 21 to October 15, 1858, Lincoln and Douglas argued about many issues but focused primarily on slavery. Douglas pressed his doctrine of popular sovereignty, while Lincoln took a fairly moderate stance, admitting that he hated slavery but did not feel that African-Americans were fully equal to whites. Lincoln moderated his views in an attempt to dilute Douglas's charges that Lincoln was a "radical" who supported racial equality. In the end, Lincoln lost the election, but many leading Republicans had been impressed with Lincoln's performance during the Great Debates and began considering him for the Republican nomination for president in 1860.

Lincoln won the Republican nomination, and in November of that year was elected sixteenth president of the United States. In Lincoln's first inaugural address, he spoke to leaders in the South who had been talking about seceding from the Union and who now called Lincoln the "diabolical leader" of "Black Republicanism."[4] As the radical abolitionists within the Republican Party had become more powerful, the South began to worry that a Republican administration might abolish slavery and destroy their social and economic way of life. Lincoln was fully aware of the South's discontent, but he downplayed the seriousness of the so-called "fire-eaters" who wanted secession. After all, the South had been threatening to secede for a long time.

In his inaugural speech, Lincoln tried to mollify Southern fears by taking a moderate stance on the slavery issue. He claimed that as president, he had no constitutional right to interfere with state social institutions such as slavery. But he was less moderate in his response to Southern threats about secession. He made it clear that he would consider any move to secede from the Union an act of rebellion, and would put it down by force if necessary. Putting down an armed rebellion, he said, was a war power granted to the president by the Constitution. Lincoln said to the South, "In your hands, my dissatisfied fellow countrymen, and not in mine, is the momentous issue of civil war."[5]

The Secession Crisis

In spite of Lincoln's conciliatory words, his inaugural speech set off the first wave of secession that included the states of South Carolina, Mississippi, Florida, Alabama, Georgia, Louisiana, and Texas. The states of Virginia, Arkansas, North Carolina, and Tennessee would eventually follow, and together they formed what they thought of as a separate nation called the Confederate States of America, with Jefferson Davis, a former senator from South Carolina, as president. The seceded states believed that Lincoln and the Republican Party were going to outlaw slavery. Indeed, Republican abolitionists had become increasingly vocal about their disapproval of the South's social and economic systems.

Of course, slavery was not the only cause of the war, although it was often at the root of other problems. Another conflict occurred between those who favored states' rights—who believed that the states had the authority to determine their own domestic institutions and secede from the Union if dissatisfied, for example—and those who believed in nationalism and the superior authority of the federal government. Another conflict was economic— the South's agrarian way of life was eventually being eclipsed by industrialism in the North. Northerners complained that the South's ebbing economy would one day become a drain on the nation, while Southerners resented any intrusion into their long-established economic and social systems. Finally, many commentators blamed the secession conflict on hotheads from the North and South. To be sure, neither radical abolitionists nor fire-eaters had ever seemed willing to compromise with one another.

Lincoln immediately sought to establish a moderate position in dealing with the secession crisis, whatever its causes. He had promised to squash the rebellion, but he was reluctant to use force prematurely, still hoping that he could convince the rebel states to rejoin the Union. As usual, Lincoln's approach provoked criticism from both sides of the political spectrum. Some radical members of his own party were in favor of allowing the Southern states to secede. Other radicals thought Lincoln should have come down harder on the South, and they urged him to suppress the rebellion with immediate force. Finally, many conservative Democrats sympathized with the South and criticized the president for opposing secession, believing that the Constitution gave the states the right to self-determination.

Lincoln himself believed that the Union was perpetual, and he argued that the states had not really left the Union—in fact, he argued that they could not—but had merely gotten out of their proper alignment with the federal government. He contended that secession was unconstitutional because it threatened to destroy the Union. Therefore, in his mind, honoring the Constitution meant saving the Union, even if that meant putting down by force an armed rebellion in the South. But the president hoped to avoid such a conflict and continued to attempt to mollify the fire-eaters. When a crisis at Fort Sumter, in March 1861, threatened to usher in civil war only one month after Lincoln took office, the new president was immediately forced to put his moderate stance to the test.

The Fort Sumter Plan

One of the promises that Lincoln had made in his first inaugural address was to hold all federal posts in Southern states should the rebellion occur. When the first states seceded, therefore, his administration had ordered Union troops to retain possession of post offices, forts, armories, and other federal properties that were being seized by Confederate troops. Lincoln believed it was important to hold these properties in order to maintain a federal presence in the South. The decision to hold onto federal strongholds was fraught with difficulty, however. This became apparent on March 5, 1861, when Major Robert Anderson notified Washington that Fort Sumter in Charleston Bay, South Carolina, was running out of provisions and would have to be abandoned. Lincoln faced a dilemma. If he ordered troops to shoot their way into Fort Sumter in order to provision the garrison, the North would criticize him for starting a war and the South would unite against an aggressive enemy. If he abandoned the fort, his actions would be considered a sign of weakness, and the embryonic Republican Party would lose credibility. Thus, Lincoln needed to devise a plan that would succeed in provisioning the fort without incurring the wrath of North or South.

With the help of Captain Gustavus V. Fox, Lincoln drew up a characteristically middle-of-the road plan. He did not send in additional troops to protect the fort—which would surely be met with armed resistance—nor did he abandon it. Instead, Lincoln decided to send only provisions to the fort and to notify South Carolina governor Francis Pickens of his plan in order to lower the risk of misunderstanding and conflict. Predictably, however, Lincoln's decision concerning Fort Sumter generated intense condemnation from both sides of the political spectrum. Many radical abolitionists criticized Lincoln for not doing more to protect the fort. Some Democrats castigated the president for not surrendering the fort to avoid conflict with the South. Even Lincoln's cabinet strenuously objected to the idea, predicting that it would provoke the South into starting civil war.

Lincoln's cabinet proved prophetic. When Governor Pickens heard of the plan to provision Sumter, he ordered his troops to fire on the fort on April 12. Lincoln's plan to relieve the hungry men holed up in the garrison was a complete failure—the supply ships never arrived at the harbor—but he did avoid having the Union fire the first shot of civil war. Viewing Pickens's attack on Sumter as an act of war, Lincoln immediately called for seventy-five thousand men to join the Union Army. As a result of the South's action at Fort Sumter, a wave of war hysteria and patriotism swept the North. The nation was now embarking on civil war, the most horrible kind of war, where neighbors kill neighbors and brothers kill brothers.

Although the Union had a larger population and seemed destined to win the war against the Confederacy, early success proved elusive. Confederate general Robert E. Lee was an able commander and the South proved resolute. The war that many thought would be over in a few months dragged on for four years and cost over 600,000 lives.

Commander-in-Chief

At Fort Sumter, Lincoln's competence as commander-in-chief of the army and navy had been put to an immediate test. Not everyone agreed that he had shown himself a capable tactician, but he did demonstrate the kind of commander he would be throughout the war. Indeed, Lincoln took an active part in the war effort, especially at the beginning of the war. Lincoln spent most of his time by the telegraph machine where he would read messages from the field about the status of battle preparations and would fire back messages indicating what he wanted done. Needless to say, his hands-on approach to running the war prompted many critics to argue that his meddling was actually hampering the war effort. No one could have agreed more with this assessment than Lincoln's general, George McClellan.

Almost immediately it became clear that McClellan and Lincoln approached military strategy differently. Lincoln was eager to end the war as soon as possible and constantly urged the cautious McClellan to move forward and confront the enemy. Again, Lincoln was questioned on all sides.

The radicals wanted Lincoln to discharge McClellan and appoint a general who would be more aggressive. Conservatives who were sympathetic to the maligned general accused the president of usurping the power of his commanders, who knew more about war than he did. Lincoln did relieve McClellan, and later the general ran unsuccessfully against Lincoln in the 1864 presidential election.

Due to the exigencies of war, Lincoln was forced to make many decisions such as the ones about Sumter and McClellan that angered representatives in Congress and large portions of the civilian population as well. On September 24, 1862, for example, Lincoln issued a proclamation suspending the writ of habeas corpus. The writ is designed as a protection of civil rights, enabling anyone who is arrested to ask for a hearing during which the justness of the arrest is decided. By suspending the writ, Lincoln eliminated citizens' protection against unlawful arrest. Lincoln took this drastic step because he believed the civil courts had become too crowded—and some had shown too much sympathy toward the South—to process writs in a timely and fair way. As a result, the courts frequently released prisoners pending trial. Most of the prisoners affected by Lincoln's decision were those arrested for interfering with the Union war effort—such as speaking against the military draft or dealing in contraband—and Lincoln thought that if they could not be held in military prisons they would simply return to their anti-war activities.

Opposition to Lincoln's decision was swift and vociferous. Critics from conservative Democrats to abolitionists accused him of taking away important civil rights. The high profile case involving Clement Vallandigham, who was arrested for speaking out against the war, especially provoked criticism. Denied the writ of habeas corpus, Vallandigham was sent to a military prison, but was later pardoned by President Lincoln and released. The military prisons themselves were another source of complaint.

They were inhospitable places where many prisoners went hungry. However, whenever Lincoln was informed about ill treatment of individual prisoners, he immediately came to their aid by ordering increased provisions or even releasing them.

Although the suspension of the writ of habeas corpus generated criticism, quotas and conscription generated even more fervent opposition. In July 1863, riots protesting Lincoln's enactment of mandatory quotas for the draft broke out in New York City. As the war dragged on, Lincoln was forced to draft more and more men for service, and his establishment of quotas for the draft turned out to be the decision for which he was most criticized by ordinary citizens. It was partly due to this criticism that Lincoln had originally conceived of a plan to issue what he called the Emancipation Proclamation, which freed the slaves of those who were in rebellion and encouraged the freedmen to join the Union army. Lincoln knew that the Union war effort was failing and that the army desperately needed more men. Getting slaves to help, the president reasoned, would only be possible if there was something in it for them, namely, freedom.

The Emancipation Proclamation

Although Lincoln had long argued that his only goal in engaging in civil war was to save the Union, he eventually had to address the main cause of the war, slavery. In August of 1862, Lincoln exchanged open letters with New York *Tribune* editor Horace Greeley about emancipation. In his letter, the president clearly stated his views about slavery. He said that he would free all of the slaves if that would save the Union, or he would free none of the slaves if that would save the Union. In other words, Lincoln made it clear that his only constitutional authority and legitimate aim was to save the Union—the abolition of slavery was ancillary to that. However, Lincoln added, "I have here

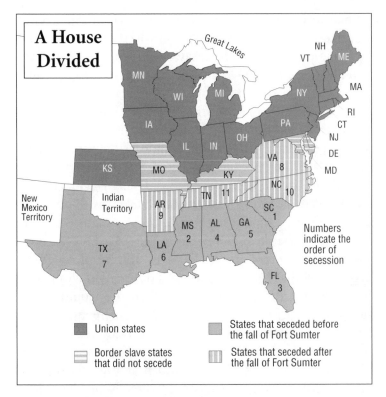

A House Divided

Great Lakes

Numbers indicate the order of secession

- Union states
- Border slave states that did not secede
- States that seceded before the fall of Fort Sumter
- States that seceded after the fall of Fort Sumter

MN, WI, MI, NY, NH, VT, ME, MA, RI, CT, NJ, IA, PA, OH, IL, IN, DE, MD, KS, MO, KY, VA 8, NC 10, New Mexico Territory, Indian Territory, AR 9, TN 11, SC 1, MS 2, AL 4, GA 5, TX 7, LA 6, FL 3

stated my purpose according to my view of official duty; and I intend no modification of my oft-expressed personal wish that all men every where could be free."[6]

The issue of slavery was so divisive that Lincoln was assaulted on all sides when he acted or failed to act to abolish slavery. Radical Republicans wanted immediate and total emancipation. Conservative Democrats wanted the Union saved without eliminating slavery. Most citizens were against social equality for African-Americans and would doubtless have not supported a war waged solely for emancipating the slaves. Whenever Lincoln acted against slavery in any way, he was immediately vilified by those who argued that he had no constitutional authority to do so. When the president held back and refused to act against slavery, radicals accused him of protecting the "evil institution."

Before issuing the Emancipation Proclamation, Lincoln had addressed the slavery issue on several occasions. He had proposed a compensated, gradual emancipation plan to Congress on March 6, 1862, which he hoped would persuade the border states to free their slaves in exchange for pecuniary aid. Lincoln believed his plan would dash the Confederacy's hopes to win over the border states and thus encourage them to surrender. The border states did not go for the plan, however. Lincoln also revoked proclamations by Union generals John C. Frémont and David Hunter which freed slaves in Confederate states held by their troops, arguing that his generals had no constitutional right to free the slaves. On August 14, 1862, Lincoln proposed a plan to colonize freed slaves in Central America. He believed that the two races would never get along and that African-Americans should go where they could set up their own society. Like compensated emancipation, however, Lincoln's colonization scheme received little enthusiasm. Finally, Lincoln signed into law the Confiscation Acts of August 6 and July 17, 1862, which allowed the federal government to liberate slaves used directly by Confederates in their war effort.

On September 22, 1862, Lincoln finally decided to take a step that he believed would help the Union war effort. As usual, when Lincoln issued the preliminary Emancipation Proclamation, he was both praised and excoriated. Radicals accused the Proclamation of not going far enough toward freeing the slaves. They pointed out that the Proclamation—merely a war document—would cease to be in effect once the war was over, leaving the fate of thousands of slaves undecided. On the other hand, Democrats accused the Proclamation of being too radical, arguing that Lincoln had no constitutional authority to free slaves under any circumstances. Many maintained that only the states had the legal right to declare slavery illegal within their boundaries. Two days after the preliminary Proclamation was issued, the Chicago *Times* published an editorial saying, "we protest against [the Emancipation Proclamation] as a monstrous usurpation, a criminal wrong, and an act of national suicide."[7]

Conversely, many praised the Emancipation Proclamation for being an important step toward total emancipation. Supporters praised Lincoln for staying within his constitutional rights by issuing an order on emancipation using his war power as commander-in-chief. On September 24, 1862, the Illinois *State Journal* argued that the Proclamation would help end the war: "President Lincoln has at last hurled against rebellion the bolt which he has so long held suspended."[8] Supporters believed that although the war document was indeed limited in scope and time, slavery would never survive it. Indeed, African-Americans all over the country celebrated the Proclamation and looked at it as their key to freedom.

Victory at Last

Although Lincoln's strongly held views about slavery encouraged him to issue the Proclamation, his main purpose was more immediately practical. The Emancipation Proclamation would allow freed slaves to join the Union army to fight against Confederate soldiers. As Union casualties mounted, winning the war against the South had become increasingly difficult. In fact, the stalemate threatened to cost Lincoln his bid for re-election in 1864. In addition, Lincoln knew that any act toward emancipation would please many European nations whose people abhorred slavery and had criticized the United States for its reluctance to give up the institution. At one point in the war, the government of Great Britain was on the verge of recognizing the Confederacy in an effort to keep Southern cotton sailing into English ports, but it had shied away from doing so because English citizens disapproved of slavery. Having issued the Emancipation Proclamation, Lincoln predicted that the

European people would not now permit their governments to help the South. Lincoln's predictions about the effects of the Emancipation Proclamation proved correct: With the help of freed slaves, the Union army was able to defeat the Confederates and finally end the war in April 1865.

Of course, Lincoln knew that the Proclamation was more than a practical war document—he believed it helped put an end to slavery in the United States forever. As he signed it, he said, "If my name ever goes into history, it will be for this act, and my whole soul is in it."[9] Lincoln also knew that when the war ended, much more was needed to end slavery permanently. He believed that since the people re-elected him in 1864 knowing his personal feelings against slavery, they were giving tacit approval for any steps that he might take to end it. Knowing that the Constitution did not grant the legislative or executive branch the authority to interfere with slavery, Lincoln favored a constitutional amendment abolishing it. However, support in Congress for the Thirteenth Amendment was lacking. When the amendment had previously gone before Congress, the Republican Senate approved, but the Democratic majority in the House voted it down. In 1865, the same Congress was still in session, and Lincoln knew that if he waited for the next Congress—which would have a Republican majority in the House—to meet, the Thirteenth Amendment would not be passed for more than a year. Impatient, Lincoln decided to approach some of the Democrats who were leaving office at the end of the session and convince them to vote for the Amendment. Lincoln's plan was successful, and on January 31, 1865, the Thirteenth Amendment to the Constitution was passed by Congress. The states ratified the Amendment on December of that year, eight months after Lincoln's assassination.

It was a cruel irony that Lincoln did not live to see the Thirteenth Amendment ratified by the states. The president had sacrificed much to save the Union and prepare the people for that Amendment. Comparing a photo taken of Lincoln when he first took office in 1861 with one taken toward the end of the war in 1865, the toll of the war on Lincoln is manifest. He went from a young man to an old one in just four years. For those four years, he did little else but deal with problems of war, an effort that exacted high personal costs. He suffered incessant criticism from all sides, and frequently lapsed into severe bouts of depression.

After his efforts on behalf of emancipation and after the Union was saved, many hailed Lincoln as the greatest president of all time—yet, typically, not everyone looked at Lincoln as a hero. Many Southerners blamed Lincoln for both the war and the devastation the South had suffered as a result. His proposals to help rebuild the South also met with controversy. Reintegrating the Southern states into the Union had proved to be a contentious affair. Several years of rancorous debate between the president and the radicals in Congress had not produced any plan that promised success. Abolitionists criticized Lincon's 10 Percent Plan, which aimed to quickly reintegrate the Southern states by allowing rebel states that obtained oaths of allegiance from 10 percent of their voters to be admitted to the Union. The radicals argued that the plan did not provide enough security for freed slaves. Among those who despised Lincoln and viewed him as a tyrant was the Confederate John Wilkes Booth.

The Assassination

Booth sat in the audience as Lincoln gave what would turn out to be his last public speech on April 11, 1865. In his address to the crowd that was celebrating General Robert E. Lee's surrender to General Ulysses S. Grant at Appomattox, which marked the end of civil war, Lincoln looked ahead rather than back. Lincoln declared Confederate president Jefferson Davis's attempt at government defunct and spoke of the federal government's responsibility to reconstruct the nation. Booth was angered at Lincoln's dismissal of the South and what appeared to the young actor as the president's move toward radicalism. When Lincoln admitted that he would prefer that the reconstructed state governments give freed slaves the vote, Booth turned to a companion and said, "that means nigger citizenship. Now, by God, I'll put him through. That is the last speech he will ever make."[10]

Booth made good on his promise. On Good Friday, April 14, 1865, Booth slipped into Lincoln's private box at Ford's Theater with his co-conspirator Lewis Thorton Powell and shot Lincoln in the back of the head. As Lincoln slumped over, Booth jumped down onto the stage and yelled, "*sic semper tyrannis*," Latin for "Thus always to tyrants."[11] Powell wounded Lincoln's Secretary of State William H. Seward. Seward survived, but Lincoln did not. On the morning of April 15, Lincoln died.

As the nation grieved, and a manhunt for Booth formed, people began to formulate theories on why the actor had shot Lincoln. Some believed Booth was simply crazy, while others thought he was part of a plan hatched by conspirators in Lincoln's own cabinet. Many analysts thought Booth was an agent of Jefferson Davis's Confederacy, and, in fact, Davis was imprisoned for two years on false charges of participating in a plot to assassinate the president. Historians now believe that the most likely explanation is that Booth's was simply a political crime like most assassinations are—he killed Lincoln because he thought the South would be better off without him. Booth was later shot and killed while trapped in a burning barn.

Lincoln's Legacy

Lincoln has been immortalized at the Lincoln Memorial in Washington, D.C., as a great American hero. On the memorial, an inscription reads: "In this temple, as in the hearts of the people for whom he saved the Union, the memory of Abraham Lincoln is enshrined forever." Harriet Beecher Stowe, author of the anti-slavery novel *Uncle Tom's Cabin*, wrote of Lincoln,

> Surrounded by all sorts of conflicting claims, by traitors, by half-hearted, timid men, by Border States men, and Free States men, by radical Abolitionists and conservatives, he has listened to all, weighed the words of all, waited, observed, yielded now here and now there, but in the main kept one inflexible, honest purpose, and drawn the national ship through.[12]

Not everyone is convinced of Lincoln's heroism. Lincoln's war to save the Union exacted a terrible price. Not only did he lose his own life, but many others lost their lives as well. In all, more than 620,000 soldiers—260,000 rebels and 360,000 Yanks—died, as well as an unknown number of civilians. According to historian James M. McPherson, the Civil War's cost in American lives was as great as in all of the nation's other wars combined through Vietnam. The South's economy and social structure were destroyed, and Reconstruction did little to help ease racial tensions or integrate freed slaves into white society. For all of these costs many have blamed Lincoln.

Indeed, conflict still surrounds Lincoln's presidency, and his character remains elusive. Because he strove to steer down the middle road, it has been difficult to determine what his real beliefs were. Many of his contemporaries viewed him as a guileless rube while others saw him as a crafty politician who manipulated the prejudices of people in order to further his own political career. To the people most committed to ending slavery, Lincoln was a reluctant emancipator, but to those who wanted to preserve slavery, he was a tyrant. Some critics thought he used the war as an excuse to violate civil rights and the rights of the states, while others commended him on always acting safely within the authority granted to him by the Constitution. Many commentators characterize Lincoln as a compassionate man committed to peace who found it necessary to use violence. By any account, however, if Lincoln's aim was "that government of the people, by the people, for the people, shall not perish from the earth," it can be safely said that he succeeded. Lincoln's legacy is indeed a difficult one to assess, and the conflict that plagued Lincoln throughout his entire political career continues still, over one-hundred and fifty years after his death.

Notes

1. Quoted in Andrew Delbanco, ed., *Portable Abraham Lincoln*. New York: Viking, 1992, p. 295.

2. Quoted in James M. McPherson, *Battle Cry of Freedom: The Civil War Era*. New York: Oxford University Press, 1988, p. 28.

3. Quoted in Delbanco, *Portable Abraham Lincoln*, p. 89.

4. Roger Bruns, *Abraham Lincoln*. New York: Chelsea House, 1986, p. 78.

5. Quoted in Delbanco, *Portable Abraham Lincoln*, p. 195.

6. Quoted in Delbanco, *Portable Abraham Lincoln*, p. 239.

7. Herbert Mitgang, *Abraham Lincoln: A Press Portrait*. Chicago: Quadrangle Books, 1971, p. 304.

8. Mitgang, *Abraham Lincoln: A Press Portrait*, p. 306.

9. Quoted in Jim Hargrove, *Abraham Lincoln*. Chicago: Children's Press, 1988, p. 11.

10. Quoted in McPherson, *Battle Cry of Freedom: The Civil War Era*, p. 852.

11. Quoted in Bruns, *Abraham Lincoln*, p. 123.

12. Quoted in Bruns, *Abraham Lincoln*, p. 120.

CHAPTER

1

THE OUTBREAK
OF CIVIL WAR

Averting Civil War: Lincoln Should Have Supported the Crittenden Compromise

David M. Potter

The Crittenden Compromise was introduced to the U.S. Senate by Senator John Crittenden two months after Abraham Lincoln was elected president in 1860. Like the Compromise of 1850 before it, the Crittenden Compromise proposed to limit, but not abolish, slavery. In spite of wide support from both Northern and Southern representatives, however, the plan was voted down in Congress in 1861, and efforts to resuscitate the spirit of compromise failed.

The main opponent to compromise was President-elect Abraham Lincoln, according to Professor David M. Potter. Potter contends that if Lincoln had supported the Crittenden Compromise, the measure would have passed. In the following excerpt, taken from his book *Lincoln and His Party in the Secession Crisis*, Potter argues that passage of the Crittenden resolutions was the key to avoiding civil war, if only temporarily. Even though the plan would not have resolved the slavery issue, he argues, adopting the measure would have forestalled armed conflict. Writing in 1962, Potter contends that peace—even if temporary—is always better than war.

THE CRITTENDEN RESOLUTIONS REPRESENTED A POSSIBLE basis for compromise. . . . The Crittenden Plan commanded a great deal of support both in the North and in the South—so much, in fact, that if Lincoln had supported it, it might have been adopted. I still think the evidence is impressive, and I still believe that if Lincoln had supported the Compromise it might have been adopted.

An Alternative to War

This, of course, means that I believed there was a possible alternative to war in 1861. It does not mean that I regarded the crisis as an artificial one, or the sources of sectional antagonism as being in any sense superficial. It does not mean that I subscribed to the doctrine that conflict was "needless" or "repressible," for . . . [as I have asserted before], "the slavery issue was certain to arouse emotions which no compromise could pacify—therefore it was beyond compromise." Yet to say that the fundamental source of friction was bound to cause deep antagonism is not, I think, the same as to say that this antagonism had inevitably to take the form of armed combat, and it is certainly not the same as to say that it had to take the form of armed combat at an exact time—April 1861—no sooner, no later.

The Crittenden Compromise had many of the same qualities and the same limitations as the Compromise of 1850. The chief limitation was that it did not and could not settle the slavery question. But within this limitation, it was perhaps less heavily freighted with bones of potential controversy than the Compromise of 1850. At least, it contained no Fugitive Slave Law [which required Northerners to return escaped slaves to the South], and it did not hold any such built-in ambiguities as later made the formula of popular sovereignty a source of chronic conflict. Perhaps it had almost as much popular backing at the beginning of 1860 as the Compromise of 1850 commanded at the beginning of the earlier year. Perhaps, also, it would have been a stopgap, or, as some would say, a "mere stopgap." The Compromise of 1850 is now widely regarded as such a stopgap; yet there is some question whether it failed in its own provisions or whether it was undone by the repeal of the Missouri Compromise in 1854 [a set of U.S. laws adopted in 1820 to maintain the balance between slave and nonslave states].

I am very reluctant to dismiss Crittenden's plan as a stopgap so long as we maintain a double standard on the subject of stopgaps. For our evaluation of them depends very much upon whose gaps are being stopped. Thus no *modus vivendi* with the Soviet Union can be much more than a stopgap in 1962, given our basic disagreements with

The Irrepressible Conflict: Why Compromise Was Doomed to Fail

Many historians reject the idea that Lincoln could have avoided Civil War by compromising with the separationists in Congress. In this excerpt from his book, And the War Came, *Professor Kenneth M. Stampp portrays the Republican anti-slavery radicals as unwilling to compromise on their conviction that slavery was wrong.*

Republican anti-slavery radicals *believed* in the doctrine of the "irrepressible conflict" and denied that it could be removed by any feasible compromise; they insisted that their platform, so far from being sectional, actually contained the only true formula for national well-being. Republicans stood by their principles, explained one, simply "because *they know their principles to be essential to the welfare and even to the very existence of the Union.*" Abolitionist James Russell Lowell encompassed the thoughts of this group precisely:

... It is quite time that it should be understood that free-that country. But we would be prone to regard it as most praiseworthy to defer a showdown, even for as much as five years. Our attitude is not unrelated to the fact that this would assure us of five years of immunity from being killed by the Russians. It is quite true, no doubt, that if war had been averted in 1861, it would not have meant a settlement of the issues. It would only have meant an indeterminate interval of immunity from being killed by the Rebs or the Yanks, as the case may be—immunity specifically for those who were killed between 1861 and 1865. Since all of these individuals would be dead by now even if the Rebs or the Yanks had not killed them, we can afford to be very bland about how right it was that the issue was met

dom is also an institution deserving some attention in a Model Republic, that a decline in stocks is more tolerable and more transient than one in public spirit, and that material prosperity was never known to abide long in a country that had lost its political morality. The fault of the Free States in the eyes of the South is not one that can be atoned for by any yielding of special points here and there. Their offence is that they are free, and that their habits and prepossessions are those of Freedom. Their crime is the census of 1860. Their increase in numbers, wealth, and power is a standing aggression. It would not be enough to please the Southern States that we should stop asking them to abolish slavery,—what they demand of us is nothing less than that we should abolish the spirit of the age. . . . It is time that the South should learn . . . that the difficulty of the Slavery question is slavery itself,—nothing more, nothing less. It is time that the North should learn that it has nothing left to compromise but the rest of its self-respect.

Kenneth M. Stampp, *And the War Came: The North and the Secession Crisis, 1860–61*. Chicago: University of Chicago Press, 1965.

in 1861, and was not put off. All I suggest is that historians who believe so zealously in the virtue of facing up to issues in the past ought not to believe in the expedients of peace in the present. If an interval of peace, without any fundamental solution of issues, is worth something today, it was worth something in 1861. In 1861, as today, it would be worth a great deal less than a real peace—a real settlement of the basic issues.

Those who despise the advantages of a stopgap peace will point out, of course, that the Civil War did settle the basic issues. It saved the Union, and it freed 4,000,000 slaves. Certainly this is true, and it is important. But it can hardly be said that these immense values were gained at a bargain. For every six slaves who were freed, approximately one soldier was killed; for every ten white Southerners who were held in the Union, one Yank or one Reb died. A person is entitled to wonder whether the Southerners could not have been held and the slaves could not have been freed at a smaller per-capita cost. Certainly few would have purchased these gains at the time if they had known the price, and the mere fact that it has already been paid is not a reason for historians to let it go without questioning now.

Both Sides Open to Compromise

The so-called revisionists, who have been most explicit in questioning the necessity for the war, have stressed certain themes: namely that the Republicans were quite prepared to guarantee the continued existence of slavery in all the slave states, and that the difference between what the Republicans proposed to do about slavery and what the Democrats proposed to do was not worth a war (this is, of course, very different from saying that slavery was not worth a war); that North and South had formed unreal, emotional stereotypes of one another, and that the opposing groups fought against these illusory stereotypes, rather than against one another; and that the war resulted from a breakdown of reason and would not have happened if reason had prevailed. In connection with these themes, they have been severely criticized for their moral indifference concerning slavery; for their failure to perceive that overwrought emotions and exaggerated stereotypes are the reflex rather than the cause of deep antagonisms; and for the fallacy that irrational forces are unreal forces. On all of these counts, it seems to me that revisionism is vulnerable, though it by no means follows that everyone associated with revisionism is open to these criticisms. . . . I do not think that a compromise averting war in 1861 would have solved the basic issues or cleared up the basic problem any more than the Compromise of 1850 did. I certainly do not think the issues or the antagonisms were in any sense unreal, nor of anything less than major importance. If I believe there was an alternative course available in 1861, it is not because I am abstractly converted to the power of rationality but because the concrete evidence seems to me to show that a majority in the South did not want disunion and that a majority in the North did not want to press the question of slavery in the territories. . . . Let me merely point out that in the election of 1860 the combined vote for Douglas and Bell in the slave states exceeded the vote for Breckinridge, and that the combined vote for Stephen A. Douglas, John Bell, and John Breckinridge in the states which stayed with the Union exceeded the vote for Abraham Lincoln. Over all, Lincoln received almost precisely the same proportion of the popular vote in 1860 that Herbert Hoover received in 1932 (39.9% and 39.6%). The evidence further seems to me to show that the Crittenden proposals commanded so much support in 1861 that if the President-elect had thrown his weight in the balance for them rather than against them, they would have been voted in Congress. If this had occurred, the fire-eating secessionists would still have resisted them bitterly, but again the evidence indicates that the fire-eaters almost failed to carry their program anyway, and if the Crittenden proposals had been thrown into the balance against them, they could hardly have gained the minimum support which they needed and which they only barely gained as it was. The Southern Unionists had beaten them in 1850 and might have done so again.

This, of course, would not have solved the ultimate problem. It would have resulted only in temporary peace. But what peace is more than temporary? Peace is essentially finite and temporal, and can be gained only by installments—not in perpetuity. Our peace with the Soviet Union . . . has never appeared more than temporary, and indeed future historians may say that it was not worth our while to preserve such a tenuous peace. If it has any merit, it is only the merit of being better than war, and that is the merit which peace in 1861 might have had.

Lincoln's Handling of the Political Battle That Led to the Civil War

Frank van der Linden

Abraham Lincoln took office in 1861 in the middle of a political firestorm. On the one side were moderate Republicans who disliked slavery but wanted to curtail the secession crisis and preserve the Union. In another camp were radical Republican abolitionists. Some abolitionists wanted to force the seceded states to return to the Union while others wanted to let them go. Lincoln also had to contend with Southern Democrats who generally supported slavery and urged conciliation with the South.

According to Frank van der Linden, Lincoln decided to remain loyal to his party and adopt the course of aggression that had been promulgated by many radical Republicans. In the following speech delivered at the National Archives in Washington, D.C. on May 19, 1999, van der Linden argues that Lincoln's decisions were distorted by political pressure. The president could have averted war, van der Linden asserts, but Lincoln believed that if he did not attempt to hold on to federal posts such as Fort Sumter in the South, their loss would ruin the Republican party. In consequence, Lincoln ordered the provisioning of Fort Sumter in spite of the protestations of his cabinet that such a course would result in civil war. Van der Linden maintains that the goals of saving the Union and emancipation could have been achieved without bloodshed. Van der Linden is a historian, former White House correspondent, syndicated columnist, and

Reprinted from "The Road to War," Frank van der Linden, a speech delivered at The National Archives, Washington, D.C., May 19, 1999. Used with permission.

author of the book, *Lincoln: The Road to War*, from which this speech was adapted.

———————■———————

I SHOULD CAUTION YOU AT THE OUTSET THAT YOU WILL FIND my portrait of Lincoln . . . is quite different from the usual picture of the serene and god-like figure brooding at the Lincoln Memorial. Those who worship at this shrine are shocked that anyone would dare say that Lincoln ever made a mistake. To them, it's like committing some sacrilege like denying the divinity of Christ. However, I am only questioning the divinity of Lincoln.

Actually, I'm following President Lincoln's own admonition to Congress in December, 1862 when he said: "As our case is new, we must think anew and act anew. . . . Fellow citizens, we cannot escape history."

So I have tried to "think anew" and "act anew" in my research, and today you will hear some new facts that you have never read in your standard history book. But be assured, they are all true, and based upon years of research in primary sources, such as letters, diaries, newspapers and the *Congressional Globe,* that period's version of the congressional *Record.* And fortunately that material was available only a short distance from here at the Library of Congress and here in the National Archives.

I am confident that you will not be like the individual who said, "My mind is made up; don't confuse me with facts."

The Civil War: A Political Conflict

Basically, I treat the conflict that we know as the American Civil War as primarily political; and the first part of my book provides enlightening details of the wheeling and dealing by various characters in the election campaign of 1860. Lincoln won the presidency by sweeping nearly all the electoral votes in the North but he had only 39 per cent of the total popular vote.

Lincoln ran almost a million votes behind the combined votes of his three opponents—Stephen A. Douglas, John C. Breckinridge and John Bell. All three urged him to follow a course of conciliation towards the South, but he rejected pleas that he make some soothing statement to reassure the Southerners who were afraid that he would enforce his anti-slavery platform and spread social turmoil all over the South.

Lincoln brushed aside the secession talk as "humbug." He said the crisis was just artificial panic stirred up by bold bad men who were trying to bully him.

When Lincoln arrived in Washington, D.C. from Springfield, Illinois, in late February, 1861, he found that secession was real. Seven states, making up a bloc from South Carolina to Texas, had pulled out and set up their own republic at Montgomery, Alabama. The fire-eaters—the radical, ruthless secessionists—were high-pressuring eight other slave states to jump aboard the secession train, too.

Lincoln's aim should have been to hold those eight reluctant states of the Upper South and thus stop the secession train on the track. His own Attorney General, Edward Bates of Missouri, wrote in his diary: ". . . in several of the misguided states of the South a large portion of the people are really lovers of the union." A reaction to the secession drive has already begun, he said. "If encouraged by wise, moderate and firm measures on the part of this government . . . the nation will restored to its integrity without the effusion of blood."

In his Inaugural Address March 4, 1861, Lincoln made an ironclad pledge that frightened the South when he said: "The power confided in me will be used to hold, occupy and possess the property and places belonging to the government."

He also told the Southerners: "In your hands, my dissatisfied fellow countrymen, and not in mine is the momentous issue of civil war. The government will not assail you. You can have no conflict without yourselves being the aggressors."

Crisis at Fort Sumter

On his first day in the White House, Lincoln suffered a shock: a letter from Major Robert Anderson, commander at Fort Sumter, saying that his food and supplies were running low and that, unless resupplied, he must give up the Charleston fort within a few weeks.

Attorney General Bates recorded in his diary that the Cabinet members were astonished to receive this bad news and "it will take a force of 20,000 men, at least, and a bloody battle, to relieve it."

General Winfield Scott, the army commander, agreed that it was a military necessity to abandon Fort Sumter. All the Cabinet members except one—Postmaster General Montgomery Blair of Maryland—went along with this decision on the night of March 9.

Two days later, on March 11, General Scott drafted an order directing Major Anderson to "engage suitable water transportation and peacefully evacuate Fort Sumter so long gallantly held—and with your entire command embark for New York."

The very next day, March 12, surgeon Samuel Wylie Crawford of the Fort Sumter garrison wrote in his diary the report that "we are to be withdrawn" because the Lincoln administration "thinks this is preferable to civil war. . . . It is said that General Scott has telegraphed that we are to be withdrawn."

But for days thereafter, the official order never came.

The reason for this delay was this:

Montgomery Blair waged a furious fight inside the Cabinet to reverse it.

He brought his brother-in-law, Gustavus V. Fox, to see

Lincoln. Fox, a former naval officer, laid out a plan to bring troops and supplies into Fort Sumter aboard several small boats, escorted by warships. Fox proposed that three tugs should slip into Charleston harbor by night: the first one would draw fire from the rebel guns; then the escorting warships could help the fort's gunners in firing back, and the war would be on.

Finding much opposition to his scheme, Fox went to Charleston as a presidential agent, ostensibly on a peaceful mission but actually to see the lay of the land—how his little ships could come in.

A few days later in March, Ward Hill Lamon came to Charleston as a "confidential agent" of his old friend, Abe Lincoln. Lamon told Governor Francis W. Pickens that he had come to arrange for a ship to remove the garrison from Fort Sumter.

Pickens said no U.S. warship would be allowed into the harbor but an ordinary steamer could take out the troops and they could retire with full military honors.

Surgeon Crawford, in his diary, quoted the governor as saying Lamon "promised to return at once with orders for the evacuation of the fort." But he never returned.

William H. Seward, the Secretary of State, kept on trying to make Lincoln order the evacuation of the fort. He felt so confident of success that he sent word to the Confederacy that the fort would be given up by about the middle of March.

Seward used a go-between—Supreme Court Justice John A. Campbell, a strong pro-Union man from Alabama—to convey his messages to the three commissioners whom Confederate President Jefferson Davis had sent to Washington on a peace mission. Lincoln refused to see the commissioners, for fear that the meeting would look like official recognition of the Confederacy. However, the New York *Herald* said Lincoln made a "big mistake" because an informal chat might have led to "a future reconstruction of the Union and peace" but "the opportunity was malignantly and stupidly thrown away."

Fort Sumter: A Political Symbol

Throughout the early weeks of March, Major Anderson confidently expected to receive General Scott's order directing him to take his troops out of Fort Sumter. But Lincoln still held back, because he could not bring himself to suffer the political abuse that would follow such a humiliating surrender. While the fort had little strategic value, it was still a powerful political symbol right there in the heart of cocky South Carolina, which had started the secession parade.

Dispatches from Washington, quoting high authorities as affirming the decision to give up Fort Sumter, appeared in major newspapers in New York, Chicago, Philadelphia, and Cincinnati. These stories may have come from Seward (they would be called "leaks" or "plants" today) to prepare the public to swallow the bitter pill.

The bad news sent a shock wave of indignant surprise sweeping through the Republicans in the North, while the Democrats gloated. Soon Lincoln received a flood of letters from angry partisans who felt betrayed. You can read these, as I did, among the Lincoln papers in the Library of Congress.

In a typical diatribe, one New York Republican told Lincoln, "You are weak and vacillating. . . . Give up Sumpter, sir, and you are dead politically. . . . You have got to either act, immediately and decisively, or resign and go home."

Republican Senators stormed into the White House and told their care-worn President that he must bravely hang onto Fort Sumter or their party would be ruined.

On March 28, Lincoln spent a sleepless night. He was torn by conflicting emotions. He yearned for peace, yet he also wanted to make a brave stand in defense of the fort; but he had received repeated warnings that this would start a civil war.

He was also sick and tired of the horde of office-seekers who were plaguing him for hours every day, demanding federal jobs. The next morning the exhausted President was "in the dumps," as he expressed it, and "keeled over" with a sick headache.

Lincoln was dangerously close to the verge of one of his bouts of deep depression.

Meeting again with his Cabinet on March 29, he finally decided that he could send food to the hungry troops at Charleston and he could label it a peaceful mission. If the rebels should attack, it would not be his fault; they must take the blame for firing the first shot.

Lincoln's Advisors Fail

On March 30, the Confederate commissioners received a telegram from Governor Pickens, asking why the federal garrison was still at Fort Sumter, long after Lincoln's man, Lamon, had positively said they would leave. Pickens felt something was not right.

The next day, Seward told Justice Campbell that Lincoln disavowed anything Lamon might have said at Charleston—that Lamon had no authority to speak for the President.

Well, Justice Campbell asked, "what shall I tell the Confederates now?"

Seward replied: "The President may desire to supply Fort Sumter, but will not undertake to do so without first giving notice to Gov. Pickens."

This development was a drastic change in policy, and the startled jurist inquired: "Does the President design to attempt to supply Sumter?"

"No, I think not," Seward answered. "It is a very irksome thing to him to evacuate it. His ears are open to everyone, and they fill his head with schemes for its supply. I do not think he will accept any of them."

The truth was that Lincoln had already sent Captain

Fox to New York to assemble the fleet that would leave for Charleston by April 6. Seward didn't mention that.

Playing his last card, Seward persuaded Lincoln to invite a leader of the proUnion men controlling the Richmond convention and offer some deal that might keep Virginia from joining the secession parade.

Abraham Lincoln the Tyrant

In the following editorial written for the Bangor Democrat *and reprinted in the* New York Evening Day-Book *on April 18, 1861, Lincoln is criticized for supporting the Republican party's efforts to stop secession. The author calls Lincoln a Tory, a name given to anyone who favored the British during the American Revolution.*

Why is [the South preparing to fight the North?] It is because that old Tory party, which under a multitude of names and disguises, first resisted the independence of America, and after its Government had become an established fact, has been unceasing in its efforts to get possession of it, and after having gained possession of it, by hypocritically assuming the sacred garb of freedom, it has undertaken to convert that Government into an instrument of tyranny, and to use all its powers to overturn the very bulwarks of liberty itself—the Sovereignty of the States. Yes, Abraham Lincoln, a Tory from his birth, is putting forth all the powers of Government to crush out the spirit of American liberty. Surrounded by gleaming swords and glistening bayonets at Washington, he sends forth fleets and armies to overawe and subdue that gallant little State which was the first to raise its voice and arm against British oppression.

"Opposition to Civil War: A Voice from Maine." *Abraham Lincoln: A Press Portrait*, ed. Herbert Mitgang. Chicago: Quadrangle Press, 1971.

John B. Baldwin came as the Virginians' agent on April 4. Lincoln led him into a White House bedroom and locked the door.

"Why do you all not adjourn the Virginia convention?" Lincoln demanded.

Baldwin said the Union men could hold onto their majority but only if "you will uphold our hands by a conservative policy." He urged Lincoln to withdraw the federal troops from both Sumter and Fort Pickens in Florida.

Baldwin warned that sending supply ships to Sumter would surely lead to war.

"Sir," he said, "if there is a gun fired at Fort Sumter, as surely as there is a God in heaven, the thing is gone. Virginia, as strong as the Union majority in the convention is now, will be out in forty-eight hours."

"Oh," said Lincoln, "that is impossible."

Baldwin later denied reports that Lincoln had offered him a deal—that, if the Virginia convention would adjourn at once without voting in favor of secession, he would withdraw the troops from Sumter. Lincoln never made such an offer for the public record.

On the same day of Baldwin's visit, several Northern governors had a long interview with Lincoln. These men—all strong Republican partisans—favored holding the forts at the cost of war. They offered men and money to support an armed conflict.

On April 8, as the fleet was moving out of New York, Robert S. Chew of the State Department arrived in Charleston by train and read to Governor Pickens this notice from Lincoln:

"An attempt will be made to supply Fort Sumter with provisions only; and that, if such an attempt be not resisted, no effort to throw in men, arms or ammunition will be made without further notice, or in case of an attack upon the fort."

So the master politician in the White House put the

Confederates in Montgomery on the spot. They could either let the ships in—or attack and be blamed for starting the war.

They offered Major Anderson a chance to give up the fort peacefully if he would set a date for his departure. He wanted to go. He dreaded the coming civil war. But he was under orders to stay while the fleet was on its way to aid him. So he had to refuse.

The First Shot

Thus, on the morning of April 12, the rebels opened fire. Their guns battered the fort for 34 hours and forced it to run up the white flag. Fortunately, no one was killed. During all the bombardment, the federal warships outside the Charleston harbor made no move to come in and help the embattled garrison. The great irony of the whole fiasco is this: the three tugs carrying most of the food never showed up. They got caught in a storm and wound up in other Atlantic ports. News of the surrender set off a wave of anger all over the North. But, when Lincoln was told that the rebels had opened fire, he did not seem shocked. He calmly remarked: "I knew they would do it."

"The plan succeeded," he told his old friend, Orville Browning of Illinois. "They attacked the fort, it fell, and thus did more service than it otherwise could."

Captain Fox was frustrated over the failure of his relief mission. Lincoln soothed him by saying: "You and I both anticipated that the cause of the country would be advanced by making the attempt to provision Fort Sumter even if it should fail; and it is no small consolation now to feel that our anticipation is justified by the results."

On April 15, Lincoln issued a proclamation calling upon the governors to provide seventy-five thousand militia men to suppress the rebellion. His call for troops ignited an explosion of patriotic fervor all over the North. The same citizens who had been crying for peace now screamed for war. In every city and town, crowds waved flags and cheered speakers who called for war upon the rebels who had dared to fire upon Old Glory. Governors in state after state telegraphed Lincoln that they would far exceed their quotas of volunteers.

By contrast, the governors of the slave states fired back telegrams to Lincoln, vowing that they would never send him any troops for the "wicked purpose of subjugating the South"; they would join in defending their states against invasion.

Lincoln's war policy completely cut the ground out from under the Union-loving men who had, for months, blocked the fire-eaters from dragging their border states out of the beloved old Union. Four more states—Virginia, North Carolina, Tennessee, and Arkansas quickly went out. So the Confederacy expanded from a weak league of seven states into a much stronger bloc of eleven states, with more men and resources to carry on a long and costly war.

Lincoln should have listened to Seward and General Scott, and let the seven cotton states alone for a few months to play at their game of creating a new nation. He could have encouraged the fire-eaters' political rivals— Union men, such as Justice Campbell—to stand firm. They could have reassured the frightened people that Lincoln really meant them no harm. The states of the upper South could have been held by conciliation, not by force, and thus the infant Confederacy would have been left with only seven states to compete with 27 in the Union, impossible odds for success.

War Could Have Been Avoided

So, in time, the Union could have been restored without bloodshed. Lincoln's announced war aim—preserving the Union—would have been achieved. Defenders of the war also praise it for abolishing slavery, which it certainly did, but at tremendous cost.

Without the war, it is true, that slavery would have remained for a long time in the Deep South, where it formed the basis of the social order. Slavery was already on the way out in the states of Delaware, Maryland, Missouri, as well as East Tennessee and Western Virginia. In time, slavery would have been ended by a constitutional amendment, but several years after the Thirteenth Amendment.

Abraham Lincoln is revered as one of our greatest Presidents, chiefly because he restored the Union and freed the slaves. Both goals were good—but they could have been achieved by a policy of peace, although, of course, it would have required more time and patience.

When anyone says the Civil War was "a good war" or "a moral war," I remember those six hundred thousand dead men and their grieving loved ones, not to mention all the thousands of wounded on both sides, the waste and the ruin of the South.

The mistakes of the past should be kept in mind and never repeated as we cope with new challenges abroad today and, once again, some voices are heard clamoring for "ground troops . . . total war," "victory," when the only real solution can come from conciliation, economic pressure and patience. And we should not forget that those who refuse to learn the lessons of history are bound to repeat its mistakes.

The Crisis at Fort Sumter: Lincoln Provoked the South into War

John Shipley Tilley

When Lincoln was inaugurated in 1861, he immediately faced a crisis when seven states in the lower South seceded from the Union. Southern posts such as Fort Sumter in Charleston Bay, South Carolina, became points of contention between the Union, which wanted to maintain strongholds in the South, and the newly formed Confederacy, which viewed such strongholds as a threat to Southern sovereignty. When Major Robert Anderson, the officer in charge of Fort Sumter, notified Washington that the fort would have to be abandoned because of dwindling supplies, Lincoln devised a plan to provision the fort. When the Southern leaders heard about Lincoln's plan, they ordered Confederate troops to fire on the fort, thus ushering in civil war.

In an excerpt from his book *Lincoln Takes Command*, history professor John Shipley Tilley contends that Lincoln deliberately provoked the war. Lincoln knew that even with forewarning the Confederates would see the provisioning of Fort Sumter as a challenge to their political autonomy and would react with aggression. Tilley maintains that Lincoln proceeded with the Fort Sumter plan in order to force the South into firing the first shot. He claims that the plan was intended to rally Northerners and wavering border states to support the Union's objective to force the seceding states back into the Union, even if it meant civil war.

W HY DID LINCOLN ADOPT A COURSE WHICH HE HAD every reason to believe would result in war?

Jefferson Davis Saw Through the Plan

As matters stood at the date of [Lincoln's] inauguration, it was obvious that [his] administration was not ready for a showdown. There were trouble-promising hurdles to clear before the track was open. For one thing, there were many in the North who openly sympathized with the Southern position; more who quailed at the suggestion of coercion of those who, rightly or wrongly believing it to be their constitutional right, were merely withdrawing from the Union. This sentiment became articulate in the outspoken proposal to let the erring sister states go out in peace. Another restraining factor loomed large; the emergency called for wide-awake handling of the border states, states with slaves, and, besides, with sharply divided loyalty. Should these cast in their lot with the seceders, there would be a decided change for the worse, but if Lincoln could devise an effective method to insure their continued allegiance, this would lessen decidedly the Southern Confederacy's prospect of success. If he could cleverly play the Southerners into committing the first overt act of hostility, he could go to the country with a far stronger appeal. Such apparently uncalled-for defiance of constituted authority would fan into flame the indignation of those not yet estranged. Then the stage would be set.

[Confederate president] Jefferson Davis saw through the plan. He knew the shrewdness of his opponent and watched the moves by which a clever trap was being laid. Knowing full well that it was likely only a matter of days when the formidable jaws would snap to, no course was open but patiently to sit and wait. Upon [Major Robert] Anderson's final refusal to surrender [Fort Sumter to the Confederates], a Confederate cabinet meeting ended in spirited disagreement as to future procedure. The ultimate responsibility was Davis' and he shouldered it:

> "The order for the sending of the fleet was a declaration of war. The responsibility is on their shoulders, not on ours. The juggle for position as to who shall fire the first gun in such an hour is unworthy of a great people and their cause. A deadly weapon has been aimed at our heart. Only a fool would wait until the first shot has been fired. The assault has been made. It is of no importance who shall strike the first blow or fire the first gun."

Partisan writers have rung the changes with a supposedly damning indictment: "The South fired the first shot." The Confederate president was not without a presentiment as to the reverberations which would follow exploitation of this fact. This he was powerless to prevent but at least he would make the Southern position clear. In the case of nations, as of individuals, he was aware, actions were to be weighed judicially only in light of antecedent aggravation. He knew that in courts of law the case of a reckless swaggerer, driven by unreasoning passion to fire first, differed materially from that of a man who luckily discovered an enemy creeping up on him with a gun. Long before, [English historian] Henry Hallam had written, "The aggressor in a war (that is, he who begins it), is not the *first* who *uses force,* but the first who renders force *necessary.*" Something akin to this the Confederate leader clearly had in mind when, later, he appealed the case to the discriminating judgment of the future:

> "The dangerous rant of demagogues about 'firing on the flag' might serve to rouse the passions of insensate mobs

in times of general excitement, but will be impotent in impartial history to relieve the Federal government from the responsibility of the assault made by sending a hostile fleet against the harbor of Charleston, to cooperate with the menacing garrison of Fort Sumter."

Davis' views, however, were those of a partisan. What thought some of Lincoln's friends and contemporaries?

Lincoln's Allies Believed He Started the War

Already familiar are the solemn warnings of [Simon] Cameron, his secretary of war, [Winfield] Scott, commander in chief of the army, and [Joseph Gilbert] Totten, the army's chief of engineers, that the course upon which he had set his heart would end in tragedy. The New York *Herald* of May 11, 1861, said, "The demonstration which precipitated the attack on Fort Sumter was resolved upon to prove to the country and the world the true character and nature of the rebellion." Quoting this, George Lunt, the Massachusetts historian, added his own comment; namely, that the purpose of the expedition was to draw the fire of the Confederates; "a *silent* aggression," he characterized it, "with the object of producing an *active* aggression from the other side." Lincoln's secretary of the navy quoted the secretary of state as observing that the attempt to hold Sumter "would be a waste of effort and energy and life, would extinguish all hope of peace, and compel the Government to take the initiative in hostile demonstrations."

What of the views of Northern writers who have made intensive study of the events of the period? John T. Morse, Jr., a biographer of Lincoln, wrote that the president "finally gained his point in forcing the Confederacy into the position of assailant, and there is every reason to believe that he bought that point cheaply at the price of the fortress." [Thornton K. Lothrop,] the writer of a life of [William Henry] Seward made this comment, "The Sumter expedition failed of its ostensible object, but it brought about the Southern attack on that fort. The first gun fired there effectively cleared the air . . . and placed Lincoln at the head of a united people."

[Lincoln secretary John] Nicolay lived in the White House and was Lincoln's intimate and confidant. It was his view that the Sumter expedition placed the Confederacy in a dilemma. If they fired on it they would thereby alienate their Northern sympathizers; if, after the determined stand they had taken, they backed down when the time arrived for action, such a surrender of principle would chill the enthusiasm of the South. He knew that Lincoln was under no illusion as to the consequences of his course. He tells much in a single sentence: "The presence of armed ships with the expedition and their instructions to fight their way to the fort in case of opposition, show that he believed the arbitrament of the sword to be at hand." As well as his chief, Nicolay knew the wisdom of a course the ultimate result of which would be a more widespread conviction that the Southerners were in the wrong. Observing that [Gustavus V.] Fox reminded the president that but nine days remained for him to reach Charleston from New York, and that this limitation of time might jeopardize his chance of success, he wrote: "But the President, who had calculated all the probabilities of failure, and who with more comprehensive statesmanship was looking through and beyond the Sumter expedition to the now inevitable rebel attack and the response of an awakened and united North, calmly assured him that he should best fulfil his duty by making the attempt."

Lincoln Admitted to Starting the War

Fortunately, for the sake of historical truth, the evidence is not restricted to views of Southerners, nor to opinions of biographers, nor to speculations of outsiders. There is a final, a more authoritative source to which resort may be made.

On April fifteenth Lincoln issued his proclamation calling for troops to suppress resistance to the laws of the United States. Fifteen days later, he wrote Fox the following letter:

"WASHINGTON, D.C., May 1, 1861
"CAPTAIN G.V. FOX. *My Dear Sir:* I sincerely regret that the failure of the late attempt to provision Fort Sumter should be the source of annoyance to you. The practicability of your plan was not, in fact, brought to a test.

"By reason of a gale, well known in advance to be possible, and not improbable, the tugs, an essential part of the plan, never reached the ground, while by an accident, for which you were in nowise responsible, and possibly I to some extent was, you were deprived of a war vessel, with her men, which you deemed of great importance to the enterprise. I most cheerfully and truly declare that the failure of the undertaking has not lowered you a particle, while the qualities you developed in the effort have greatly heightened you, in my estimation. For a daring and dangerous enterprise of a similar character you would to-day be the man of all my acquaintances whom I would select. You and I both anticipated that the cause of the country would be advanced by making the attempt to provision Fort Sumter, *even if it should fail;* and it is no small consolation now to feel that our *anticipation is justified by the result.*

"Very truly, your friend,

"A. LINCOLN"

Lincoln Did Not Deliberately Provoke War at Fort Sumter

Richard N. Current

When Lincoln took office in March 1861, seven Southern states immediately seceded from the Union. One of the first decisions the new president had to make in response to this secession crisis was what to do about Fort Sumter in Charleston Bay, South Carolina, one of the seceded states. Lincoln and other Union sympathizers wanted to keep the forts under the control of the North. When Major Robert Anderson informed Lincoln that Fort Sumter was running out of provisions and would have to be abandoned, Lincoln devised a plan that would enable the Union to maintain control of the fort. The majority of Lincoln's cabinet disapproved of the plan, fearing that any attempt to provision Sumter would provoke hostilities from the Confederates. Lincoln proceeded with the expedition, however, and his cabinet's fears proved well-founded: Confederate troops did indeed fire on the fort, precipitating civil war.

In the following selection, history professor and Lincoln scholar Richard N. Current argues that Lincoln did not deliberately provoke war with his plan to provision Fort Sumter. In an excerpt from his book *Lincoln and the First Shot*, Current maintains that Lincoln believed that a peaceable provision was possible. Current asserts that although the president recognized that his plan might provoke the Confederates into firing the first shot, Lincoln did not intentionally maneuver to have the first

Excerpted from *Lincoln and the First Shot*, by Richard N. Current (Prospect Heights, IL: Waveland Press). Copyright © 1963 by Richard N. Current. Used with permission.

shot fired. He accepted that a military response to the fort situation *might* occur, but he wanted the South to be the aggressor, not the North.

DID LINCOLN THINK, OR DID HE HAVE GOOD REASON TO think, that he could send his expedition to Sumter and his advance notice to the South Carolina governor without encountering resistance on the part of the Confederate forces at Charleston? Unfortunately, there is no direct, contemporary evidence to show what Lincoln *actually thought* about the probable Confederate reaction. There is, however, plenty of evidence to indicate what he *had good reason to think*.

A Peaceful Provisioning Was Unlikely

Lincoln was familiar with the news of recent events at Charleston—events illustrating the readiness of the Confederate batteries to open up. He knew that in January 1861 his predecessor, President James Buchanan, had sent an unescorted and unarmed merchant steamer with provisions and (below deck) troops for Sumter, and that the Charleston batteries had fired upon this vessel and compelled her to turn back. Now, Lincoln was sending not one ship but several, including warships. He had reason to expect that his expedition would meet with at least the same degree of hostility as Buchanan's had met with, if not more. Before Lincoln's expedition had actually sailed, he received confirmation of this probability in the report that, on April 3, the Confederate batteries fired upon the Boston schooner *R.H. Shannon,* which innocently had put in at Charleston Harbor to get out of the ocean fog.

When Lincoln called upon his cabinet for written advice, on March 15 and again on March 29, he got little assurance the first time and still less the second time that a peaceful provisioning would be likely. The first time only two of the seven members favored making the attempt, and only one of the two, Secretary Salmon Chase, was confident that it could be made without armed conflict. The second time only one definitely opposed the attempt, but even Chase, who still favored it, had lost his confidence that it could be carried out peaceably. Secretary Gideon Welles, who had changed from opposition to approval, now expressed an opinion similar to Chase's. "There is little possibility that this will be permitted," Welles stated, "if the opposing forces can prevent it."

The objection may be raised that, nevertheless, Lincoln had reason to think *his* Sumter expedition, unlike Buchanan's, might be tolerated by the authorities in Charleston because he intended to give, and did give, advance notice of its coming, whereas Buchanan had not done so. Though [Professor Charles W.] Ramsdell has characterized this notice as a threat, and a double-barreled one at that, his critics have replied that it was no such thing. They say it was given "to show that hostile surprise was not intended" and to make clear Lincoln's "non-aggressive purpose." Whether the notification, with its reference to "men, arms, or ammunition," constituted a threat, we need not stop to debate. We need only to recall what Lincoln had learned recently from Hurlbut, his secret emissary to Charleston. Hurlbut reported his conclusion "that a ship known to contain *only provisions* for Sumpter would be stopped & refused admittance." In the light of this information, Lincoln would have had little ground for expecting that his notice would mollify the Confederates even if he had confined it to a simple announcement that he would attempt to supply "provisions only."

If Lincoln had intended and expected nothing but a peaceful provisioning, he no doubt would have been surprised and disappointed at the actual outcome. In fact, however, he repeatedly expressed a feeling of at least qualified satisfaction and success. When he replied to the Virginia delegates at the White House, on April 13, he said in an almost triumphant tone that the "unprovoked assault" would set him "at liberty" to go beyond the self-imposed limitations of his inaugural and to "repossess" as well as "hold, occupy, and possess" Federal positions in the seceded states. When he consoled the frustrated Gustavus V. Fox, on May 1, he wrote: "You and I both anticipated that the cause of the country would be advanced by making the attempt to provision Fort-Sumpter, even if it should fail; and it is no small consolation now to feel that our anticipation is justified by the result." When he drafted his first message to Congress, for the July 4 session, he emphasized the point that, by the "affair at Fort Sumpter," he had succeeded in making good his earlier declaration that, if war should come, the seceders would have to be the aggressors.

The Provocation Theory Is Unsupported by Evidence

On July 3, 1861 [Lincoln's friend Orville] Browning recorded in his diary that he had talked with Lincoln that night and that Lincoln spoke thus as to Sumter: The plan [sending supplies] succeeded. They attacked Sumter—it fell, and thus, did more service than it otherwise could."

If this remark by Lincoln nearly three months after the event was correctly quoted and if it meant a deliberate maneuver to cause the South to fire the first shot, it is, as to Lincoln's motive, unsupported by contemporary evidence of March and April, 1861. It is significant that when two expeditions were preparing, the one that was given orders to sail and act was directed to that fort at which Southern attack was *not expected* (Pickens), while the one made "ready" in a tentative sense was concerned with the fort where trouble was more likely. The purpose of the Sumter expedition when sent was merely to maintain the status quo as nearly

And when he read the message to Browning, on July 3, he went on to remark, as Browning paraphrased him: "The plan succeeded. They attacked Sumter—it fell, and thus, did more service than it otherwise could."

Accepting Aggression Is Not the Same as Provoking It

In short, it appears that Lincoln, when he decided to send the Sumter expedition, considered hostilities to be *probable*. It also appears, however, that he believed an unopposed and peaceable provisioning to be at least barely *possible*. It is reasonable to suppose that he shared the expectation of his Attorney General, who wrote in his diary at the time Fox was leaving New York for Charleston: "One of two things will happen—either the fort will be

as possible by giving food to the garrison. Only in case of Southern attack was there to be a forcible effort to land troops. The nature of the announcement of the expedition to Southern authorities should also be noted. Had the purpose been to trick the South into firing the first shot, a leakage of information as to a supposedly secret expedition with hints as to hostile intent would have served better. Instead of this there was an official notification with emphasis upon non-hostile intent and with a pledge not to reënforce unless attacked. It would be going very far indeed to imply that this emphasis was insincere. Lincoln's note to [South Carolina] Governor [Francis W.] Pickens did not read like the message of a leader trying to induce the other side to make an assault, nor did his actions and orders in April, taken in their setting and without reading meanings back into them, indicate any such intention.

J.G. Randall, *Lincoln the President: Springfield to Gettysburg*. New York: Dodd, Meade and Company, 1946.

well provisioned, the Southrons forebearing to assail the boats, or a fierce contest will ensue." If the first rather than the second of the two possibilities had materialized, then Lincoln doubtless could have said afterwards, just as he said when the second of the two occurred, that his plan had succeeded. Doubtless he would have been equally well satisfied, perhaps even better satisfied. Either way, whether the Confederates resisted or not, he would have been (in the words of his secretaries John Nicolay and John Hay) "master of the situation." . . .

On the one hand, Lincoln did not count confidently upon peace, though he thought there was a bare chance of its being preserved for the time being. On the other hand, he did not deliberately provoke war. He thought hostilities would be the likely result, and he was determined that, if they should be, they must clearly be initiated by the Confederates. "To say that Lincoln meant that the first shot would be fired by the other side *if a first shot was fired*," as Professor J.G. Randall has most admirably put the matter, "is not to say that he maneuvered to have the first shot fired."

Lincoln's Commitment to Saving the Union

Lord Charnwood

When seven Southern states seceded from the Union in 1861, Abraham Lincoln was faced with several choices. Many radical abolitionists urged Lincoln to let the states go, arguing that compromise with Southern states over the issue of slavery would inevitably fail and cause endless strife within the nation. Others who were not opposed to slavery also argued that the Southern states were legally allowed to secede under the Constitution. Lincoln was not won over by these arguments. His main objective was to preserve the Union. Lincoln believed that if he allowed the Southern states to secede, he would weaken the bonds that held the United States together and doom the first major experiment in democracy to failure.

The English lawyer Lord Charnwood, in his book *Abraham Lincoln,* from which this excerpt is taken, takes a sympathetic view of Lincoln's opposition to secession. Charnwood argues that secession is only justified when it is founded on a moral cause. He claims that the Confederacy's aim to form a political union held together only by slavery was not moral and could not be justified. Furthermore, Charnwood commends Lincoln for opposing the forces that would have weakened and eventually destroyed the United States.

Excerpts from *Lincoln*, by Lord Charnwood, (London: Constable and Company, 1916).

I T IS IMPOSSIBLE TO AVOID ASKING WHETHER ON THE QUES-
tion of constitutional law the Northern opinion or the
Southern opinion was correct. . . . If we go behind the Constitution, which was then and is now in force, to the original document of which it took the place, we shall find it
entitled "Articles of Confederation and Perpetual Union,"
but we shall not find any such provisions as men desirous
of creating a stable and permanent federal government
might have been expected to frame. If we read the actual
Constitution we shall find no word distinctly implying
that a State could or could not secede. As to the real intention of its chief authors, there can be no doubt that they
hoped and trusted the Union would prove indissoluble,
and equally little doubt that they did not wish to obtrude
upon those whom they asked to enter into it the thought
that this step would be irrevocable. For the view taken in
the South there is one really powerful argument, on which
Confederate president Jefferson Davis insisted passionate-
ly in the argumentative memoirs with which he solaced
himself in old age. It is that in several of the States, when
the Constitution was accepted, public declarations were
made to the citizens of those States by their own representatives that a State might withdraw from the Union. But
this is far from conclusive. No man gets rid of the obligation of a bond by telling a witness that he does not mean
to be bound; the question is not what he means, but what
the party with whom he deals must naturally take him to
mean. Now the Constitution of the United States upon the
face of it purports to create a government able to take its
place among the other governments of the world, able if it
declares war to wield the whole force of its country in that
war, and able if it makes peace to impose that peace upon
all its subjects. This seems to imply that the authority of
that government over part of the country should be legally indefeasible. It would have been ridiculous if, during a
war with Great Britain, States on the Canadian border

should have had the legal right to secede, and set up a neutral government with a view to subsequent reunion with Great Britain. The sound legal view of this matter would seem to be: that the doctrine of secession is so repugnant to the primary intention with which the national instrument of government was framed that it could only have been supported by an express reservation of the right to secede in the Constitution itself.

The Duke of Argyll, one of the few British statesmen of the time who followed this struggle with intelligent interest, briefly summed up the question thus: "I know of no government in the world that could possibly have admitted the right of secession from its own allegiance." Oddly enough, President James Buchanan, in his Message to Congress on December 4, 1860, put the same point not less forcibly.

Seceding in the Name of Slavery

But to say—as in a legal sense we may—that the Southern States rebelled is not necessarily to say that they were wrong. The deliberate endeavour of a people to separate themselves from the political sovereignty under which they live and set up a new political community, in which their national life shall develop itself more fully or more securely, must always command a certain respect. Whether it is entitled further to the full sympathy and to the support or at least acquiescence of others is a question which in particular cases involves considerations such as cannot be foreseen in any abstract discussion of political theory. But, speaking very generally, it is a question in the main of the worth which we attribute on the one hand to the common life to which it is sought to give freer scope, and on the other hand to the common life which may thereby be weakened or broken up. It sometimes seems to be held that when a decided majority of the people whose voices can be heard, in a more or less defined area, elect to live for the future under a particular government, all enlightened men elsewhere would wish them to have their way. If any such principle could be accepted without qualification, few movements for independence would ever have been more completely justified than the secession of the Southern States. . . . In the six cotton-growing States which first seceded, and in several of those which followed as soon as it was clear that secession would be resisted, the preponderance of opinion in favour of the movement was overwhelming. This was not only so among the educated and governing portions of society, which were interested in slavery. While the negroes themselves were unorganised and dumb and made no stir for freedom, the poorer class of white people, to whom the institution of slavery was in reality oppressive, were quite unconscious of this; the enslavement of the negro appeared to them a tribute to their own dignity, and their indiscriminating spirit of independence responded enthusiastically to the appeal that they should assert themselves against the real or fancied pretensions of the North. . . . Broadly speaking, it is certain that the movement for secession was begun with at least as general an enthusiasm and maintained with at least as loyal a devotion as any national movement with which it can be compared. And yet today, just fifty-one years after the consummation of its failure, it may be doubted whether one soul among the people concerned regrets that it failed. . . .

The English suspicion, that there must have been some cause beyond and above slavery for desiring independence, never had any facts to support it. Since 1830 no exponent of Southern views had ever hinted at secession on any other ground than slavery; every Southern leader declared with undoubted truth that on every other ground he prized the Union; outside South Carolina every Southern leader made an earnest attempt before he surrendered the Union cause to secure the guarantees he thought sufficient for slavery within the Union. The Southern statesman (for the soldiers were not statesmen) whose character most attracts sympathy now was Alexander Stephens, the Vice-President of the Southern Confederacy, and though he was the man who persisted longest in the view that slavery could be adequately secured without secession, he was none the less entitled to speak for the South in his remarkable words on the Constitution adopted by the Southern Confederacy: "The new Constitution has put at rest for ever all the agitating questions relating to our peculiar institution, African slavery. This was the immediate cause of the late rupture and present revolution. The prevailing ideas entertained by Jefferson and most of the leading statesmen at the time of the old Constitution were that the enslavement of the African was wrong in principle socially, morally, and politically. Our new government is founded upon exactly the opposite idea; its foundations are laid, its corner stone rests, upon the great truth that the negro is not the equal of the white man; that slavery—subordination to the white man—is his natural and normal condition. This, our new government, is the first in the history of the world based upon this great physical, philosophical, and moral truth. The great objects of humanity are best attained when there is conformity to the Creator's laws and decrees." Equally explicit and void of shame was the Convention of the State of Mississippi. "Our position," they declared, "is thoroughly identified with slavery."

Lincoln's Election Endangered the Future of Slavery

It is common to reproach the Southern leaders with reckless folly. They tried to destroy the Union, which they really valued, for the sake of slavery, which they valued more; they in fact destroyed slavery; and they did this, it is said, in alarm at an imaginary danger. This is not a true ground of reproach to them. It is true that the danger to slavery from the election of Lincoln was not immediately pressing. He neither would have done nor could have done more than to prevent during his four years of office any new acquisition of territory in the slave-holding interest, and to impose his veto on any Bill extending slavery within the existing territory of the Union. His successor after four years might or might not have been like-minded. He did not seem to stand for any overwhelming force in American politics; there was a majority opposed to him in both Houses of Congress; a great majority of the Supreme Court, which might have an important part to play, held views of the Constitution opposed to his; he had been elected by a minority only of the whole American people. Why could not the Southern States have sat still, secure that no great harm would happen to their institution for the present, and hoping that their former ascendancy would come back to them with the changing fortunes of party strife? This is an argument which might be expected to have weighed with Southern statesmen if each of them had been anxious merely to keep up the value of his own slave property for his own lifetime,

Preserving the Democratic Experiment

On July 4, 1861, Lincoln addressed Congress in special session. In his speech, Lincoln outlined the events that led to civil war, articulated his justification for invoking the presidential war power against the South, and requested that Congress legally acknowledge war against the seceded states. In the following excerpt, the president argues that he had no choice but to use force in order to preserve the world's first experiment in democracy.

And this issue [of violent secession] embraces more than the fate of these United States. It presents to the whole family of man, the question, whether a constitutional republic, or a democracy—a government of the people, by the same people—can, or cannot, maintain its territorial integrity, against its own domestic foes. It presents the question,

but this was far from being their case. It is hard for us to put ourselves at the point of view of men who could sincerely speak of their property in negroes as theirs by the "decree of the Creator"; but it is certain that within the last two generations trouble of mind as to the rightfulness of slavery had died out in a large part of the South; the typical Southern leader valued the peculiar form of society under which he lived and wished to hand it on intact to his children's children. If their preposterous principle be granted, the most extreme among them deserve the credit of statesmanlike insight for having seen, the moment that Lincoln was elected, that they must strike for their institution now if they wished it to endure. The Convention of South Carolina justly observed that the majority in the North had voted that slavery was sinful; they had done little more than express this abstract opinion, but they had done all that. Lincoln's administration might have done apparently little, and after it the pendulum would probably have swung

whether discontented individuals, too few in numbers to control administration, according to organic law, in any case, can always, upon the pretences made in this case, or on any other pretences, or arbitrarily, without any pretence, break up their Government, and thus practically put an end to free government upon the earth. It forces us to ask: "Is there, in all republics, this inherent, and fatal weakness?" "Must a government, of necessity, be too *strong* for the liberties of its own people, or too *weak* to maintain its own existence?"

So viewing the issue, no choice was left but to call out the war power of the Government; and so to resist force, employed for its destruction, by force, for its preservation.

Abraham Lincoln, "Message to Congress in Special Session, July 4, 1861, *The Portable Abraham Lincoln*, ed. by Andrew Delbanco. New York: Viking, 1992.

back. But the much-talked-of swing of the pendulum is the most delusive of political phenomena; America was never going to return to where it was before this first explicit national assertion of the wrongfulness of slavery had been made. It would have been hard to forecast how the end would come, or how soon; but the end was certain if the Southern States had elected to remain the countrymen of a people who were coming to regard their fundamental institution with growing reprobation. Lincoln had said, "This government cannot endure permanently, half slave and half free." Lincoln was right, and so from their own point of view, that of men not brave or wise enough to take in hand a difficult social reform, were the leaders who declared immediately for secession. . . .

The responsibility for the actual secession does not rest in an especial degree on any individual leader. Secession began rather with the spontaneous movement of the whole community of South Carolina, and in the States which followed leading politicians expressed rather than inspired the general will. The guilt which any of us can venture to attribute for this action of a whole deluded society must rest on men like John C. Calhoun, who in a previous generation, while opinion in the South was still to some extent unformed, stifled all thought of reform and gave the semblance of moral and intellectual justification to a system only susceptible of a historical excuse.

A Nation Dedicated to the Inequality of Men?

The South was neither base nor senseless, but it was wrong. To some minds it may not seem to follow that it was well to resist it by war, and indeed at the time, as often happens, people took up arms with greater searchings of heart upon the right side than upon the wrong. If the slave States had been suffered to depart in peace they would have set up a new and peculiar political society, more truly held together than the original Union by a single avowed principle; a nation dedicated to the inequality of men. It is not really possible to think of the free national life which they could thus have initiated as a thing to be respected and preserved. Nor is it true that their choice for themselves of this dingy freedom was no concern of their neighbours. We have seen how the slave interest hankered for enlarged dominion; and it is certain that the Southern Confederacy, once firmly established, would have been an aggressive and disturbing power upon the continent of America. The questions of territorial and other rights between it and the old Union might have been capable of satisfactory settlement for the moment, or they might have proved as insoluble as Lincoln thought they were. But, at the best, if the States which adhered to the old Union had admitted the claim of the first seceding States to go, they could only have retained for themselves an insecure existence as a nation, threatened at each fresh conflict of interest or sentiment with a further disruption which could not upon any principle have been resisted. . . . It is inaccurate, though not gravely misleading, to say that the North fought against slavery. It would be wholly false to say that they fought for mere dominion. They fought to preserve and complete a political unity nobly conceived by those who had done most to create it, and capable, as the sequel showed, of a permanent and a healthy continuance.

Lincoln's Patriotism

And it must never be forgotten, if we wish to enter into the spirit which sustained the North in its struggle, that loyalty for Union had a larger aspect than that of mere allegiance to a particular authority. Vividly present to the mind of some few, vaguely but honestly present to the mind of a great multitude, was the sense that even had slavery not entered into the question a larger cause than that of their recent Union was bound up with the issues of the war. The Government of the United States had been the first and most famous attempt in a great modern country to secure government by the will of the mass of the people. If in this crucial instance such a Government were seen to be intolerably weak, if it was found to be at the mercy of the first powerful minority which seized a worked-up occasion to rebel, what they had learnt to think the most hopeful agency for the uplifting of man everywhere would for ages to come have proved a failure. This feeling could not be stronger in any American than it was in Lincoln himself. "It has long been a question," he said, "whether any Government which is not too strong for the liberties of the people can be strong enough to maintain itself." There is one marked feature of his patriotism, which could be illustrated by abundance of phrases from his speeches and letters, and which the people of several countries of Europe can appreciate today. His affection for his own country and its institutions is curiously dependent upon a wider cause of human good, and is not a whit the less intense for that. There is perhaps no better expression of this widespread feeling in the North than the unprepared speech which he delivered on his way to become President, in the Hall of Independence at Philadelphia, in which the Declaration of Independence had been signed. "I have never," he said, "had a feeling politically that did not spring from the sentiments embodied in the Declaration of Independence. I have often pondered over the dangers which were incurred by the men who assembled here and framed and adopted that Declaration of Independence. I have pondered over the toils that were endured by the officers and soldiers of the army who achieved that independence. I have often inquired of myself what great principle or idea it was that kept the Confederacy so long together. It was not the mere matter of separation of the colonies from the motherland, it was the sentiment in the Declaration of Independence which gave liberty, not alone to the people of this country, but I hope to the world, for all future time. It was that which gave promise that in due time the weight would be lifted from the shoulders of all men."

How Lincoln Justified the War: From Preserving the Union to Abolishing Slavery

Kenneth M. Stampp

When Lincoln took office in March 1861, he had to decide how to handle the secession crisis. He basically had three choices: he could try to compromise with the seceding states, he could let them go, or he could force them to return. Always an advocate for self-determination in other countries, Lincoln nevertheless decided to use military means to force the seceded states back into the Union, effectively denying them their right to self-determination. As Kenneth M. Stampp explains in the following selection, Lincoln justified his decision by stating that his primary duty as a representative of the American people was to maintain the Union. However, Stampp argues that as the war went on and casualties began to rise, Lincoln began to feel that saving the Union was insufficient justification for a war that had exacted so high a price. According to Stampp, Lincoln eventually came to embrace emancipation as the moral cause that could justify such a bloody civil war. Kenneth M. Stampp is a professor of history at the University of California, Berkeley, and former president of the Organization of American Historians. He has written several books on the Civil War era, including *The Peculiar Institution* and *America in 1857: A Nation on the Brink*.

Excerpts from "The United States and National Self-Determination," by Kenneth M. Stampp, from *Lincoln the War President: The Gettysburg Lectures*, edited by Gabor S. Boritt. Copyright © 1992, 1994 Gabor S. Boritt. Used by permission of Oxford University Press, Inc.

THE UNITED STATES HAS A LONG TRADITION—NOT UN-mixed, of course, with self-interest—of sympathy for movements abroad which sought to vindicate the doctrine of national self-determination—if I may use a twentieth-century term for a nineteenth-century nationalist concept. . . .

However, I wonder what the public response would be if the question of self-determination should arise as an American *internal* issue, as it now presents itself in many other nations, including our Canadian neighbor. Canada confronts the problem in French-speaking Quebec, whose gradually escalating demands for autonomy may yet culminate in a movement for full independence. The Canadian government has elected to deal with the problem peacefully through negotiation, and a resort to a violent resolution at present appears unlikely.

The idea that such a problem might one day confront the United States government might seem preposterous, but since the future is unpredictable a little speculation may be justified. Suppose the large Spanish-speaking population in Florida, or southern Texas, or southern California continues to grow until it becomes in one or another of these regions a governing majority. Suppose also that within this population ethnic consciousness increases and grievances and resentments accumulate, culminating, as in Quebec, in a movement for political autonomy. Would the tradition of self-determination prevail, or would a second tradition—the one seated at [the Battle of] Appomattox after the loss of 600,000 American lives—be invoked? Abraham Lincoln defined the second tradition succinctly in his first inaugural address: "I hold, that in contemplation of universal law, and of the Constitution, the Union of these States is perpetual. . . . Continue to execute all the express provisions of our national Constitution, and the

Union will endure forever—it being impossible to destroy it, except by some action not provided for in the instrument itself." In short, as the South learned at a terrible price, self-determination was not applicable to the federal Union. Apparently there was one tradition for export, another for use at home. . . .

As late as the 1820s the general view of the Union as an experiment still persisted, and the alleged right of secession had not yet been challenged by a systematic argument affirming the perpetuity of the Union. Nevertheless, the state of the Union had by then changed significantly. Its practical economic value was widely understood. Moreover, during and after the War of 1812, a strong sense of nationhood and pride in American citizenship had developed. The United States did not escape the current of romantic nationalism that was sweeping over the Western world. The time was ripe for a new conception of the federal Union as an absolute good. . . .

Nationalism vs. Secession

Although the term "self-determination" was not in use in the 1860s, southern secession was in essence an assertion of that right. But this movement had its oddities. First, the three million enslaved blacks, the Confederacy's true ethnic minority and its most severely oppressed population, had no voice in the matter and no reason to support secession. Second, white Confederates, in spite of their claim that they had become a distinct and separate people, had no ethnic characteristics to distinguish them from Northerners—no notable differences in language, religion, political traditions, or population origins, and few unique traits to give them a clear cultural identity. Rather, at the core of the white South's drive for independence was its perception of Lincoln as a threat to its slave labor system and its conviction, based on racial fears, that emancipation would be an economic and social catastrophe. The "immediate cause" of secession, according to Alexander H. Stephens, Vice President of the Confederacy, was slavery. In the Confederate government, he avowed, "its foundations are laid, its cornerstone rests, upon the great truth that the negro is not equal to the white man; that slavery . . . is his natural and moral condition."

When northern nationalists were at last convinced that the disunionists were in earnest, they ridiculed the constitutional justification of peaceful secession as a feeble argument long since discredited. Southern ordinances of secession, in Lincoln's blunt words, were "insurrectionary or revolutionary, according to circumstances." As for the *right* of revolution, proclaimed by Thomas Jefferson, that drastic course could be justified only in a struggle *against* oppression, not in its defense. The Philadelphia *Press* doubted that any revolution was ever commenced "on more trifling and trivial grounds" than those advanced by the South. . . .

Lincoln Accepts War to Preserve the Union

President-elect Lincoln shared the determination of the "stiff-backed" Republicans to defend the Union, whatever the cost. Soon after the election he realized that stern measures might eventually be necessary. Recognizing southern independence would be a violation of his oath of office. The President derives his authority from the people, he said, and they had not empowered him to arrange the terms for a dissolution of the Union.

In the past Lincoln had spoken eloquently in support of self-determination for Hungary and, more generally, of all people's "sacred" right of revolution. In 1848, while serving in Congress, he had said, "Any people anywhere, have the *right* to rise up, and shake off the existing government, and form a new one that suits them better." Moreover, that right is not limited to cases in which the whole people of a nation choose to exercise it. "Any portion of such people," he avowed, "*may* revolutionize, and make their *own* of so much of the territory as they inhabit." In 1861, however, when contemplating domestic rather than foreign revolution, Lincoln qualified his position. "The right of revolution," he now claimed, "is never a legal right. . . . At most, it is but a moral right, when exercised for a morally justifiable cause. When exercised without such a cause revolution is no right, but simply a wicked exercise of physical power." Lincoln thus viewed the southern rebellion as established governments have always viewed rebellion, whatever its cause—that is, as lacking the moral base required to give it validity. The true issue, he said, was not self-determination but whether "a democracy—a government of the people, by the same people—can, or cannot, maintain its territorial integrity against its own domestic foes.". . .

None was more determined than the nationalist Lincoln that the war should be waged solely to preserve the Union. Although he had long hated slavery and had asserted that the Union could not endure permanently "half slave and half free," he had never advocated the overthrow of slavery by force. In the present crisis he believed that the cause of the Union must have priority over the cause of the slave. In his message to a special session of Congress, in July, 1861, Lincoln recalled and confirmed the pledge he had made in his inaugural address: "I have no purpose, directly or indirectly, to interfere with the institution of slavery in the States where it exists." For the first two years of the war vindicating the principle of a perpetual Union remained his single goal. . . .

From Nationalist to the Great Emancipator

Even so, [Lincoln's Emancipation Proclamation—issued in its final version on January 1, 1863—], which also authorized the recruitment of blacks for the Union army, did less than justice to an act potentially so momentous in its social consequences. Apart from political expediency, the reason, in all probability, was that when Lincoln issued it he himself did not fully recognize that the conflict thereby would be transformed into a great social revolution. In his view, it was still a war for the Union, nothing more. "For this alone have I felt authorized to struggle," he assured a critic, "and I seek neither more nor less now."

What, then, caused Abraham Lincoln, the nationalist, the narrowly focused, almost obsessive defender of the Union during the war's first two years, to broaden his vision and become at last the Great Emancipator? It was hardly a role that he had anticipated. This remarkable transformation began sometime in the summer of 1863. By then the war had gone on too long, its aspect had become too grim, and the escalating casualties were too staggering for a man of Lincoln's sensitivity to discover in that terrible ordeal no greater purpose than the denial of the southern claim to self-determination. The great battles of the spring and summer of 1862—Shiloh, the Seven Days, Second Bull Run, and Antietam—had brought home to him the magnitude of the task he had undertaken. The combined Union and Confederate casualties in those four battles and in the four that followed—Fredericksburg in December, Chancellorsville in May, 1863, Gettysburg in July, and Chickamauga in September—numbered 234,000. Proportionally, in our present population, the casualties of those eight battles, fought in a period of eighteen months, would have amounted to nearly two million.

Searching for a Divine Purpose

Sharing responsibility for the events that had brought these lamentable results was more than Lincoln had bargained for when he won the presidency. As Richard Hofstadter observed in a perceptive biographical essay: "Lincoln was moved by the wounded and dying men, moved as no one in a place of power can afford to be. . . . For him it was impossible to drift into the habitual callousness of the sort of officialdom that sees men only as pawns to be shift-ed here and there and 'expended' at the will of others." Bearing this heavy burden, being a man of deeply religious temperament, it was natural for him, amid the death and destruction, to search for a divine purpose, one that per-haps he had failed to comprehend.

An early indication of Lincoln's broadening concep-tion of the war's meaning was his response to a serenade a few days after the Union victory at Gettysburg. He was not then prepared, he said, to deliver an address worthy of the occasion, but he spoke briefly and feelingly of the need to defend the principle that "all men are created equal" against those who would subvert it. He returned to that theme in his memorable Gettysburg Address, in which, near the end, another sign of his nascent vision appeared. When Lincoln expressed the hope that those who died at Gettysburg "shall not have died in vain—that this nation, under God, shall have a new birth of freedom," he was, for the first time, anticipating the imminent end of slavery as well as the preservation of the Union. It is reasonable, I think, to give an abolitionist meaning to his phrase "a *new* birth of freedom."

By the time of his Gettysburg Address, Lincoln had abandoned his public posture of indifference to the fate of southern slaves. . . . On several occasions, including his third and fourth annual messages to Congress, he vowed that he would not "retract the emancipation proclamation; nor, as executive, ever return to slavery any person who is free by the terms of that proclamation, or by any of the acts of Congress." Could such treachery, he asked, "escape the curses of Heaven, or of any good man?" By the summer of 1864, after the 86,000 Union and Confederate casualties of General Grant's Wilderness campaign, the change in Lin-coln's vision was complete, for he would no longer make peace merely on the basis of a restored Union. Fully aware of the contribution of black troops to the Union cause, he now insisted that an acceptable peace must include both "the integrity of the whole Union, and the abandonment of slavery."

In June, 1864, when the Thirteenth Amendment, providing final and complete emancipation, first came to a vote in the House of Representatives, it failed to win the required two-thirds majority. Lincoln's wholehearted support was crucial in getting that vote reversed the following January. Responding to a serenade after the passage of the amendment, he congratulated the country "upon this great moral victory." Lincoln had indeed become the Great Emancipator. . . . In a letter, dated February 13, 1865, [Abolitionist William Lloyd] Garrison commended him warmly for the part he had played in the final abolition of slavery: "As an instrument in [God's] hands," he wrote, "you have done a mighty work for the freedom of millions . . . in our land. . . . I have the utmost faith in the benevolence of your heart, the purity of your motives, and the integrity of your spirit."

Lincoln's Ambiguous Legacy

An instrument in God's hands. That seemed to be the role to which Lincoln had resigned himself when he delivered his beautiful and deeply moving second inaugural address. In this, his final effort to grasp the meaning of the war, he came full circle, for the cause of the Union now seemed ancillary to the approaching liberation of four million slaves. Perhaps it was God's will, he suggested, that the war must continue "until all the wealth piled by the bond-man's two hundred and fifty years of unrequited toil shall be sunk, and until every drop of blood drawn with the lash, shall be paid by another drawn with the sword." Lincoln spoke without malice. In his view the cause of the slave was beyond malice, the guilt of slavery was shared by all, and retribution was best left to divine judgment.

The profoundly religious sentiments expressed in the

second inaugural address were those of a man who not only had led the nation through a devastating crisis but, because of it, had experienced an unsettling personal crisis as well. The address was his testament, his witness, that, by embracing the cause of the slave, he had found the war's ultimate justification and thereby a way to come to terms with his God and with himself. Nothing less personal could explain the depth of feeling that his words revealed.

Reading Lincoln's private letters and public papers from 1848 to 1865 leaves one with the impression that on the issue of self-determination his legacy to posterity is both ambiguous and complex. In spite of his earlier defense of that principle, his nationalism and belief in the perpetuity of the Union had led him to crush the one attempt in our history to apply it at home. Secession, he affirmed, was neither a constitutional procedure nor an appropriate extralegal remedy for alleged grievances in a democracy such as ours.

That was part of his legacy. But he left unanswered the question of when, by whom, and for what cause the right of self-determination could be justifiably invoked. That question still remains unanswered. Being an internal matter, it has never been treated in international law. Woodrow Wilson's Fourteen Points only dealt with specific cases, and his more general statements were vague to say the least. The United Nations Charter commits its members to respect the principle of self-determination, but it, too, fails to establish standards by which to judge the claims of the many ethnic groups who assert their right to independence.

Historically, the success of movements for self-determination has had little to do with the justice or morality of individual cases. Success has depended on the good will of the national state involved, as may eventually be the case of Quebec; or on its inherent weakness, which has been the case of the remaining republics in the Soviet Union; or on the decisions of victorious great powers, as were the cases of Poland, Czechoslovakia, and Yugoslavia after the first World War; or on the military strength of the rebels themselves, as was the case of the United States, in alliance with France, in 1783.

In 1918, Robert Lansing, Woodrow Wilson's Secretary of State, expressed skepticism about the very principle of self-determination, believing that it was unworkable and full of mischief. Recently, historian Arthur Schlesinger, Jr., warned that the current widespread assertion of the principle is a potential threat to the unity of most national states, and that even in the United States "the outburst of multicultural zealotry threatens . . . a new tribalism." Moreover, Lansing wondered, if self-determination were a valid principle, how can we justify Lincoln's refusal to grant independence to the southern Confederacy?

However, Lincoln ultimately escaped that dilemma by attributing Confederate defeat to divine intervention on the side of a just and moral cause. In the end, when the cause of the Union no longer seemed to be sufficient, he invoked the cause of the slave, rather than the authority of the Constitution, to justify the sacrifice of so many lives. That is what makes his legacy ambiguous.

Nevertheless, if self-determination should ever again become an internal issue for the United States, it would be quite logical for us to turn to Lincoln's messages and papers for guidance. Among them we would find not only the clear imperative of his militant first inaugural address but the chastening words of his second inaugural address as well. Let us be sure, if such a time should come, that the foundation of the Union cause will be at least as just and moral as his!

CHAPTER

2

SUSPENSION OF THE WRIT OF HABEAS CORPUS

Lincoln's Temporary Dictatorship

William Archibald Dunning

In 1861, Lincoln suspended the writ of habeas corpus to allow army officers to arrest and detain without trial citizens suspected of treason. Lincoln's suspension of the writ turned out to be one of the most controversial decisions made during the Civil War. William Archibald Dunning, in an excerpt from his book *Essays on the Civil War and Reconstruction*, argues that Lincoln established a temporary dictatorship when he suspended the writ. In fact, Lincoln's decision to suspend the writ was the culmination of a series of constitutionally questionable actions that Lincoln took at the start of the Civil War as part of his approach to save the nation at whatever cost. The president received tacit approval for his actions from Congress, however, which considered such decisions as blockading Southern ports and suspending the writ necessary to save the Union. Furthermore, Lincoln was acting under the authority of the war powers granted to the president by the Constitution. Dunning was the Francis Lieber professor of political philosophy at Columbia University and president of the American Historians Society and the American Political Science Association.

THE CIRCUMSTANCES IN WHICH THE GOVERNMENT FOUND itself after the fall of Sumter were entirely unprecedented. The President was obliged to regard the uprising of

Excerpts from *Essays on the Civil War and Reconstruction*, by William Archibald Dunning, (New York: Macmillan, 1897).

the South as a simple insurrection; but the only parallel case, the Whiskey Insurrection in Washington's administration, was so insignificant in comparison, that from the very beginning a system of original construction of the constitution had to be employed to meet the varied occasions for executive as well as legislative action. Long before the end of the war, the principles thus evolved had become so numerous and so far-reaching in their application, as entirely to overshadow the most cherished doctrines of the old system. . . .

The question presented to the administration by the commencement of hostilities was: Has this government the power to preserve its authority over all its territory? The answer of the old school of constitutional lawyers was: "Yes, so far as it is conferred by the constitution and the laws"; but the answer we derive from the actual conduct of the war is "Yes" without qualification.

Immediately upon the fall of Sumter, the assertion of the new doctrine began. Before the assembling of Congress, July 4, a series of proclamations by the President called into play forces deemed necessary to the preservation of the nation. The calling out of the militia was based upon the law of 1795. . . .

The Blockade of Southern Ports

Four days after the call for militia, the President's purpose of ignoring the connection of the state governments with the rebellion was put to a severe test in his proclamation of a blockade of the ports of the Cotton States. He was obliged to speak of "the pretended authority" of those states, but only to declare that persons who, under such authority, molested United States vessels would be treated as pirates. This assumption by the executive of the right to establish a blockade was rather startling to conservative minds. It seemed like a usurpation of the legislative power to declare war. For blockade is an incident of actual warfare, and involves the recognition of belligerent rights. The constitutionality of the President's action, however, was affirmed by the Supreme Court in the Prize Cases, and hence, Congress having acquiesced, it has the sanction of all three departments of the government. Accordingly, the President, as commander-in-chief, can determine, without reference to Congress, the time when an insurrection has attained the proportions of a war, with all the consequences to person and property that such a decision entails.

Further action by the President previous to the meeting of Congress included a call for the enlistment of forty thousand three-year volunteers, and the increase of the regular army by over twenty thousand men, and the navy by eighteen thousand. Mr. Lincoln himself doubted the constitutionality of these measures.

> Whether strictly legal or not [he says, they] were ventured upon under what appeared to be a popular demand and a public necessity, trusting then as now that Congress would readily ratify them. It is believed that nothing has been done beyond the constitutional competency of Congress.

This frank substitution of a "popular demand" for a legal mandate, as a basis for executive action, is characteristic of the times. The President's course was approved and applauded. Howe, of Wisconsin, proclaimed in the Senate that he approved it in exact proportion to the extent to which it was a violation of the existing law. The general concurrence in the avowed ignoring of the organic law emphasizes the completeness of the revolution which was in progress. The idea of a government limited by the written instructions of a past generation had already begun to grow dim in the smoke of battle.

Suspending the Writ

The remaining subject dealt with in the President's proclamations was the suspension of the writ of *habeas corpus.*

Southern sympathy in Maryland had taken so demonstrative a form that summary measures of repression were resorted to by the government. General Winfield Scott was authorized by the President to suspend the writ of *habeas corpus* at any point on the military line between Philadelphia and Washington. This assertion by the executive of an absolute control over the civil rights of the individual in regions not in insurrection excited rather more criticism than the measures which would unpleasantly affect only the rebellious states. A case was promptly brought before Chief Justice Roger B. Taney for judicial interpretation. Justice Taney's opinion took strong ground against the constitutionality of the President's act. The clause of the constitution touching the matter says: "The privilege of the writ of *habeas corpus* shall not be suspended, unless when in cases of rebellion or invasion the public safety may require it." The implication is that in the cases mentioned the privilege may be suspended, but the clause is silent as to who shall do it. Precedent and authority were certainly with the chief justice in regarding the determination of the necessity as a function of the legislature. But to have awaited the meeting and action of Congress in the present case might have been to sacrifice the government. Lincoln therefore availed himself of the latitude of construction possible by the wording of the clause. Attorney-General Edward Bates sustained the President in an elaborate opinion. His ground was that in pursuance of the obligation to execute the laws, the President must be accorded the widest discretion as to means. The use of military force to suppress insurrection was authorized by the constitution, and when such means had been determined upon by the executive, all the incidents of warlike action must necessarily be included. Nor could the judicial department, being a co-ordinate and not a superior branch of the government, interfere.

The position of the executive in this matter was entirely consistent with that assumed in the establishment of the blockade. Granting the right in the President to decide when war has technically begun, both the powers in question spring naturally from the recognized authority of the commander-in-chief. In the interval between April 12 and July 4, 1861, a new principle thus appeared in the constitutional system of the United States, namely, that of a temporary dictatorship. All the powers of government were virtually concentrated in a single department, and that the department whose energies were directed by the will of a single man.

The dictatorial position assumed by the President was effective in the accomplishment of two most important results, namely, the preservation of the capital and the maintenance of Union sentiment in the wavering border states. . . .

The War Power

The question as to the extent of the government's authority over the life, liberty and property of the individual in states not in insurrection was complicated by the controversy over the proper department for exercising such authority. It has already been stated that the action of the President in suspending the writ of *habeas corpus* of his own accord in 1861 had excited a discussion of his right to do it, and that Chief Justice Taney had given an opinion against the right. The impotence of the judiciary as against the executive, and the neglect of Congress to take any action on the matter, had left the administration in a position to realize its own ideas of its powers. Arrests of disaffected persons and Southern sympathizers under secret orders from Washington had gone on without ceasing, and in no case was the service of the great writ allowed. Not only in Maryland, and the regions near the seat of war, but in the most distant parts of the land, from Maine to California, men were seized without any information as to the charges against them, and were confined in forts and prison camps. It was not denied by the friends of the policy that frightful injustice was often done, but that fact was rightly held to have no bearing on the question of power involved. If the constitution of the United States vested in the executive, in time of war, absolute discretion as to the means to be employed to carry on the war, whatever evils resulted from the exercise of this discretion must only be added to the aggregate of misery of which a resort to arms is the cause, and so must be regretted, but sternly endured.

For a year and a half after the beginning of the war the arrest and detention of citizens as "prisoners of state" went on without any formal announcement as to the principles of the proceedings. Only when, in the autumn of 1862, a draft had become necessary to recruit the army, were the government's operations put upon a well-defined basis. On September 24, a proclamation was issued by the President, ordering, first, that as a necessary measure for suppressing the existing insurrection, all persons "discouraging volunteer enlistments, resisting military drafts, or guilty of any disloyal practice affording aid and comfort to the rebels," should be subject to martial law, and liable to trial by courts-martial or military commissions; and second, that the writ of *habeas corpus* should be suspended in respect to all persons arrested or held by military authority. In this paper the President formally assumed the right to proclaim martial law and to suspend the writ of *habeas corpus* at his own discretion throughout the United States. On this assumption the power both to arrest and to detain a citizen— and, indeed, to put him to death—was complete.

Lincoln Was Right to Suspend the Writ of Habeas Corpus

J.G. Randall

The writ of habeas corpus, which guarantees the right to anyone who is arrested to ask for a court hearing to justify the cause of his or her arrest, has long been considered a bulwark against unlawful arrest and imprisonment. Thus, Lincoln's decision to suspend the writ in 1861, in an effort to squelch what he considered an armed rebellion, was highly controversial. Many Democrats and other Southern sympathizers deplored Lincoln's action as an attack on civil liberties. Others charged that only Congress had the power to suspend the writ.

University of Illinois history professor and Lincoln biographer J.G. Randall argues that Lincoln was justified in suspending the writ of habeas corpus. In the following excerpt from his book, *Constitutional Problems Under Lincoln*, Randall contends that Lincoln was mindful of the threat to civil liberties associated with his actions and suspended the writ only when he was certain it was necessary to save the Union. Randall cites the opinions of two of Lincoln's contemporaries, his attorney general, Edward Bates, and the legal pamphleteer, Horace Binney, who argue that the Constitution permits the president to suspend the writ in order to put down rebellion. Most important, Randall claims that the real issue is not who suspended the writ, but whether the action was justified. In his opinion, events in 1861 made suspension a necessary action.

Excerpts from *Constitutional Problems Under Lincoln*, by J.G. Randall (Champaign: University of Illinois Press, 1951).

T HE EXTENT TO WHICH PRESIDENT LINCOLN STOOD IN need of [the] solemn admonition [of Chief Justice Roger B. Taney—who thought the right to suspend the writ of habeas corpus belonged to Congress—] may best be judged by his attitude at the time the suspension was authorized. As a matter of fact few measures of the Lincoln administration were adopted with more reluctance than this suspension of the citizen's safeguard against arbitrary arrest. This reluctance appears in the fact that only a qualified suspension was ordered in 1861, that the military authorities were enjoined to use the power sparingly, that the action was taken during a recess of Congress, and that an early opportunity was taken to lay the matter before the special session of Congress convened for the emergency in the summer of '61.

Lincoln's Reluctance

Lincoln's secretaries [John Hay and John Nicolay] have preserved for us the original autograph draft of his message to this special session, and it is an instructive exercise to compare this draft with the revised and published form of the message. Selected portions of the earlier and later forms of the message are placed in parallel columns [see below].

Original Autograph	*Published Form*
Soon after the first call for militia, I *felt it my duty* to authorize the commanding general, in proper cases . . . to suspend the privilege of the writ of *habeas corpus*. . . . *At my verbal request, as well as by the general's own inclination, this authority has been exercised but very sparingly.* Nevertheless, . . . I *have been*	*it was considered a duty* *This authority has purposely been exercised . . . sparingly.* *the attention of the country has*

reminded from a high quarter that one who is sworn to "take care that the laws be faithfully executed" should not himself be one to violate them. Of course *I gave some consideration to the questions of power and propriety before I acted* in this matter. The whole of the laws *which I was sworn to [execute]* were being resisted . . . in nearly one-third of the States. *Must I have allowed them to finally fail of* execution? Are all the laws but one to go unexecuted, and the Government itself go to pieces, lest that one be violated? . . . *But . . . I was not, in my own judgment, driven to this ground. In my opinion, I violated no law.* The provision of the Constitution . . . is equivalent to a provision that [the] privilege may be suspended when, in cases of rebellion or invasion, the public safety does require it. . . . *I decided* that we have a case of rebellion.	*been called to the proposition, etc.* *. . . some consideration was given . . . before this matter was acted upon.* *The whole of the laws which were required to be . . . executed.* *Must they be allowed to finally fail?* *But it was not believed that this question was presented. It was not believed that any law was violated.* *It was decided, etc.*

In the original autograph one may read, as it were, the President's mental struggling at the time the decision was taken. In this remarkable document may be seen the clearest indication that the appearance of military dictatorship was a matter of deep concern to the nation's war chief and that his action was determined by what he believed to be the imperative demands of the actual situation. His course in this matter was in keeping with other acts, such as the call for troops and the blockade, in which momentous decisions had to be reached during the recess of the legislature.

In justification of his course Lincoln argued his paramount duty as chief executive to preserve the integrity of the Government, a duty on whose performance the life of the whole Constitution rested. In Lincoln's view there was no violation of the Constitution, since the Constitution permits suspension when the public safety requires it during a rebellion and does not specify what branch of the Government is to exercise the suspending power. As the provision was plainly made for an emergency, he argued, the natural inference is that the President should use his discretion, not that the danger should run its course till Congress could be called together. When the public safety does require it, the suspension is constitutional. After mature thought he decided that a rebellion existed and that the public safety did require a qualified suspension. It was therefore authorized.

Support for Lincoln's Decision

Such was Lincoln's answer to the opinion of Chief Justice Taney. For a more detailed defense of the President's course one may turn to such documents as the opinion of Attorney General Bates and the elaborate pamphlets of Horace Binney. Bates contended that the three great branches of the Government are coordinate and that the executive cannot rightly be subjected to the judiciary, as would be the case if a high executive function should be obstructed by a judicial writ. The President, he maintained, is in a peculiar manner the preserver, protector and defender of the Constitution; and it is particularly his duty to put down a rebellion because the courts are too weak to do so, while all the means of suppression are in his hands. That the President is judge of the exigency and of the manner of discharging his duty has been already held by the Supreme Court, said Bates, in an analogous case. Granted that the power opens the way for possible abuse, it is just as true that a legislature may be factious or a court corrupt.

The President cannot be required to appear before a judge to answer for his official acts. A *habeas corpus* hearing is like an appeal, and a judge at chambers cannot entertain an appeal from a decision of the President of the United States, especially in a case purely political. In spite, therefore, of the Chief Justice's decision limiting the right of suspending the *habeas corpus* privilege to the legislature, Bates contended that, as a temporary and exceptional matter in an emergency, the President has the power to order a suspension and is under no obligation to obey a writ of a court after capturing insurgents or spies. For any breach of trust, he said, the President is answerable before the high court of impeachment and before no other tribunal.

In the writings of the contemporary legal pamphleteer, Horace Binney, executive suspension finds learned support. . . .

The Vagueness of the Constitution

In the debates and records of the constitutional convention there seemed to Binney something mysterious about the *habeas corpus* clause. In his opinion there appeared to be a deliberate hushing of the subject, which was concealed as a sort of skeleton in the closet. The silence regarding such matters as executive imprisonment, the period of time during which the suspension might obtain, the nature of the offense for which the privilege might be withdrawn, the authority to suspend, and the process of warrant and arrest to be pursued all this inexactness seemed to result from a reluctance to dwell upon the subject.

The framers [of the Constitution] in Binney's view should have been more explicit, for it is a timid horseman who puts a blind upon his horse. The clause as written by [framer Charles] Pinckney had provided that the privilege should not be "suspended by the legislature except on the most urgent and pressing conditions and for a limited time not exceeding —— months." (The number of months was left blank.) Later Gouverneur Morris moved the clause practically as it now stands while the powers of the judiciary were under consideration. It was the Committee on Style and Arrangement which grouped it with the clauses concerning Congress. Thus, according to Binney, the word legislature was "struck out" and the clause as it stands is a substitute for Pinckney's wording which would have placed the power with Congress.

In determining which department has the power to suspend, the vital question, as Binney saw it, is as to which department is more particularly charged with care for the public safety. Does it require an act of Congress, he asked, to declare that a rebellion or invasion exists? No, it is the President's power and duty to decide the existence of a rebellion. So far as the calling out of the militia is concerned, this fact has been fully established, as in the 1794 Whisky Rebellion [when the militia was called to put down an uprising of citizens angry at the new whiskey tax], the *Martin vs. Mott* decision, and on other occasions. In an actual rebellion or invasion the declaration and proclamation of the fact rest unquestionably with the executive, and no other department could appropriately decide the fact. What is true as regards the calling of the militia is equally true concerning the suspension of the *habeas corpus* privilege, for considering the methods and devices of rebellion, open and covert, the power of suspending is a most reasonable attribution to the executive power. History, it was pointed out, attests the justice of this interpretation, for during the time of the Burr conspiracy [when Aaron Burr tried to detach the Western states and the Louisiana Territory from the Union in 1804] the Senate, from motives of partisanship, passed a bill suspending the privilege for three months in the case of men who had committed treason, nothing being said of rebellion or invasion. From this may be argued the unwisdom of leaving such a function to Congress.

It is a mistake, said Binney, to assume that the Constitution authorized only such things as can be carried into effect by statute. In this matter of withdrawing the writ, the Constitution takes the place of the English Parliament. The Constitution itself, by clear implication legalizes the suspension. "The Constitution does not authorize any department of the Government to authorize it. The Constitution itself authorizes it.". . .

A Presidential Function

To reach an over-all judgment on this historic controversy is not a simple matter. Judging by the views of many Congressmen, the flood of pamphlets, the learned words of Taney, and the pronouncements of lower courts, the weight of opinion would seem to incline to the view that Congress has the exclusive suspending power; and many would doubtless insist that this is the accepted American principle. But in a similar crisis the presidential power to suspend would probably be just as much a potential function as during the Civil War. As to the actual precedent of that war, the outstanding fact is that the Chief Executive "suspended the writ," and that, so far as the legal consequences were concerned, he was not restrained in so doing by Congress nor by the courts.

Even where Congress authorizes the suspension, the actual putting into force of such suspension is a presidential function, exercised by proclamation. If the procedure of 1871 were to be followed, the most essential function would still be left with the President, for Congress in that case empowered the President to suspend the privilege "whenever in his judgment the public safety shall require it," thus leaving the actual suspension to the President, with discretion to act within the limits indicated by the statute.

Since the suspension of the privilege is a "condition, not an act," it would also be necessary for the President to declare the restoration of the privilege—in other words, to terminate the suspension. This again would involve an exercise of presidential discretion. In no case, therefore, can the presidential function be entirely ignored; and there would appear to be an essentially executive quality in the whole proceeding. In the case of President Ulysses S. Grant [who sent troops into South Carolina in 1871 to take possession of arms and arrest resisters], Congress took the initiative, but in many instances—perhaps in the typical ones—the President would necessarily have to take the initiative, and under such circumstances the Lincoln precedent would naturally be invoked.

The silence of the Constitution was perhaps fortunate as the event proved, for in more than a century and a half under the Constitution the only general suspension occurred at a time when the Government was controlled by an administration highly regardful of individual rights and yet forced by circumstances to adopt summary measures. It was Horace Binney's view that the framers erred in making the language indefinite, but one may well ask whether a specific provision on such a point would not have been more of a hindrance than a help. Considering the rareness of the exercise of the power, and the lack of abuse of it, it might seem to many that the constitutional omission was really a case of golden silence, and that the brevity and flexibility of the clause pertaining to *habeas corpus* was an advantage.

After all, the essential question is not who suspends, but whether the emergency actually calls for summary arrest, and whether the rule of necessity is observed in the taking and holding of prisoners. If due restraints are observed during the period of suspension; if it is merely a "suspension" and not a setting aside of guarantees; if the withholding of the writ is not taken as equivalent to the establishment of martial law or as a justification of summary execution, then no serious outrage upon American sensibilities is likely to be threatened.

Lincoln Reluctantly Carried Out a Policy of Repression

Dean Sprague

After Lincoln suspended the writ of habeas corpus in 1861, the number of arbitrary arrests of people accused of treason began to increase. Those suspected of working up anti-Union sentiments and feeding the rebellion were detained indefinitely without trial in federal forts and military prison camps. According to the following excerpt from history professor Dean Sprague's book *Freedom Under Lincoln*, the president carried out this policy of repression with great reluctance. When the war began, Sprague claims, the president preferred that arbitrary arrests not occur, but as the crisis deepened, Lincoln came to recognize them as necessary to preserve the Union. Nevertheless, Lincoln made sure prisoners were treated humanely, and he waived or commuted sentences whenever possible.

━━━━━━

T HE YEAR 1861 WAS PERHAPS THE MOST EXCITING IN AMER- ican history. Not only did it witness such dramatic events as the firing on Fort Sumter and the emergence of two great American nations at war, but it also saw a political cloud descend over the North, causing the temporary obliteration of the traditional American system of due process of law. In handling the problem of loyalty, the entire judicial system was set aside. The laws were silent, indictments were not found, testimony was not taken, judges did not sit, juries were not empaneled, convictions were not obtained and sentences were not pronounced. The Anglo-Saxon concept of due process, perhaps the greatest political triumph of the ages and the best guardian of freedom, was abandoned.

Political Events and the Balance of Power

The constitutional safeguards against convictions for treason seemed to be too stringent. As one federal judge in New York told a grand jury in November, 1861: "Words, oral, written or printed, however treasonable, seditious or criminal by themselves, do not constitute an overt act of treason, within the definition of the crime." Many indictments were brought in the federal courts, but usually the cases were continued from one term to the next and eventually dismissed by the government. One authority who studied this matter concluded that "in the midst of . . . disloyalty . . . the tribunals of civil justice failed, in the large sense, to function as agencies for the suppression and punishment of treason." The problem was so new and the necessary alteration in the balance of power between the states and federal government so great, that it could be made only through summary action.

And so, the political steps necessary to preserve the American nation were taken by the Lincoln Administration. For Abraham Lincoln, who seemed so frequently to let his subordinates run the government, never allowed them to stray far from his major goals. He was prepared to make every sacrifice to save the Union and the arbitrary arrests [made under the suspension of the writ of habeas corpus] were, in his opinion, part of the necessary sacrifice.

During 1861, two great political events occurred which preserved the Union. The first was the detachment of three slave states from the Confederacy and their firm anchoring to the Union. Without success in this effort, the war could not have been won. These three states, Maryland, Missouri and Kentucky, not only occupied highly strategic positions, but they had a combined population of approximately three million people. Without them the population advantage of the North over the South would have been only 3-to-2, which probably would not have been enough to support the massive Union campaigns of brute force by which the South was eventually destroyed. With them, however, the proportion was 5-to-2, and made possible almost any human attrition without seriously jeopardizing the North's position. The South was in such a serious situation by the end of 1861 that it must lose the war unless the North's will could be blunted.

The second major political achievement in 1861 was the unification of the free states by the federal government. No war could be fought and won by a weak executive against the odds that faced the North. And so States Rights, which prior to 1860 had been as important a part of northern political beliefs as southern, were overturned to meet the crisis. The North would be more than an alliance of independent states. By the end of 1861, a radical transformation in the balance of political power within the North had occurred. This was accomplished through the policy of repression more than by any other action and it was Lincoln's success here which insured that the North's will to win would not be blunted.

A Policy of Repression

In carrying out the policy of repression, President Lincoln was a man caught in an agony. The first comments that he wrote on the subject epitomized his attitude: "Unless the necessity for these arbitrary arrests is *manifest,* and *urgent,* I prefer they should cease." He was forced to do something that he hated to do, since he felt it was necessary for the preservation of the Union. Nevertheless, his personal intercession again and again was in the direction of leniency. When the question of arresting the Maryland legislature first came up in April, 1861, he decided against it. When it was reported that one of the prisoners was in bad health, he ordered that his confinement be "mitigated so far as it can be consistently with his safe detention." When he heard that conditions were bad in Fort Lafayette [where prisoners accused of treason were kept without trial], he directed the United States marshal in the vicinity of the forts to "supply decent lodgings and subsistence for such prisoners."

When Senator William M. Gwin and two others from California were arrested and brought to Washington for an interview, the President decided that "they might go their several ways, they to ask no questions nor any questions to be asked of them and the pending affairs . . . to be thus entirely disposed of and ended." When James W. Wall was in prison, he wrote to Lincoln: "Permit me to lay before you how deeply I am impressed with your exceeding great kindness in extending to my wife and little ones your unrestricted permission to visit me at this place. . . . An act of kindness like that you have just performed touches the generous sympathies of my heart with great power."

"Mr. Lincoln doesn't believe in hanging," said the New York *Times*. A later writer said that "Lincoln used this power with discretion and forbearance. . . . He was the most humane man that ever wielded such authority. He had no taste for tyranny."

Despite his great leniency, he was a man of iron who was willing to see hundreds of thousands of young men die for the sake of the Union and not above sending a few hundred to prison for opposing the war. Repeatedly, whenever Congress asked for information on the arrests, he replied that it was not in the public interest to furnish the information. Furthermore, he formally suspended the writ of habeas corpus in progressively larger areas as the war continued. This fact, plus a few highly publicized cases, such as the arrest of

Clement L. Vallandigham, which occurred later in the war, made it appear that the policy of repression was being enlarged.[1] But such was not the case. Had Vallandigham been arrested in September, 1861, when he was a member of Congress, the occurrence would have rated scarcely a paragraph in the newspapers. When he was actually arrested two years later, after he had lost his seat in Congress, he became a national celebrity. By this time, the famous knock on the door at midnight had become a rare event.

The desire of President Lincoln to avoid the arrests, and the agony they caused him, never changed. But in 1861 he believed them necessary to preserve the Union. After a few months of experience in sending men to Fort Lafayette, however, he became convinced that this power could safely be used sparingly. During the rest of the war, he never changed his opinion. For President Lincoln had gone through the valley of the shadow during 1861 and had emerged a stronger man and the nation a stronger nation. Great disasters and terrible defeats lay ahead as the war moved toward a climax, but the President was never again thrown into a panic such as the one he lived through in 1861. With his slow, sure tread, he moved away from the policy of repression and the North was spared the omnipresent shadow of Fort Lafayette.

The Supreme Court Settles the Issue

The ultimate legal question of arbitrary arrest and imprisonment was settled the year after the war in the case of *Ex parte Milligan*, in which the Supreme Court held that in the absence of actual invasion such actions were illegal while civil processes were unobstructed and the courts in session. In language which has echoed to our own time, the Court held that "the Constitution of the United States is a law for rulers and people, equally in war and in peace, and covers with the shield of its protection all classes of men, at all times, and under all circumstances."

It is not difficult to imagine Abraham Lincoln nodding in agreement, had he lived, when the Court added that "during the late wicked Rebellion, the temper of the times did not allow that calmness in deliberation and discussion so necessary to a correct conclusion" on this question. For no one had regretted the acts more than he, and when the war was over and the Union saved, the prairie lawyer who became President would probably have sought, with the Court, to prevent his successors from following this dangerous precedent.

Notes

1. On May 6, 1863, Clement L. Vallandigham was convicted of uttering disloyal opinions in an attempt to weaken the power of the Federal government to suppress the rebellion. Vallandigham's request for a writ of habeas corpus was denied, and many criticized Lincoln's repressive policies. Lincoln commuted Vallandigham's sentence from imprisonment to banishment.

Lincoln's Repression of Civil Liberties Has Been Exaggerated

James M. McPherson

Democrats during Lincoln's time and many historians in subsequent decades have criticized the sixteenth president for suspending the writ of habeas corpus at the start of the Civil War. However, professor James M. McPherson contends that the repression of civil liberties that occurred under Lincoln's administration was mild compared to the draconian measures adopted in America's subsequent wars. In his book *Ordeal by Fire: The Civil War and Reconstruction*, McPherson argues that Lincoln was justified in suspending the writ of habeas corpus. Civilian courts would have been slow to handle the increasing numbers of cases, he claims, and would have been forced to release prisoners pending trial, enabling those convicted to return to their anti-Union activities. Furthermore, McPherson notes that the federal government endured much criticism without retaliation and conducted free elections for the duration of the Civil War. McPherson is Edwards professor of American History at Princeton University and author of *The Struggle for Equality* and *Battle Cry of Freedom: The Civil War Era*.

———

TWO DAYS AFTER SIGNING THE EMANCIPATION PROCLAMA-tion, Lincoln issued a second edict; this one suspended the writ of *habeas corpus* and authorized the military arrest of "all Rebels and Insurgents, their aiders and abettors within the United States, and all persons discouraging volunteer enlistments, resisting militia drafts, or guilty of any disloyal practice."[1] Democrats denounced this action as the tyrannical twin of emancipation. The two proclamations provided the opposition with its main issues in the 1862 congressional elections. It is necessary to examine the question of civil liberties in the wartime North. . . .

Arbitrary Arrests

During 1861 the State Department was responsible for enforcing internal security. [Secretary of State William H.] Seward organized a secret service network of agents and informers whose zeal frequently exceeded their discretion. The government arrested hundreds of men in the border states and detained them without trial. In Maryland, federal troops imprisoned several members of the legislature and a state judge. The army also arrested and punished numerous spies, saboteurs, and guerrillas in the occupied portions of the South and border states.

By executive order in February 1862, Lincoln transferred responsibility for all internal security matters to the War Department. [War Secretary Edwin M.] Stanton reduced the number of arrests and established a commission to examine the cases of prisoners then being held. Most of them were released upon taking an oath of allegiance. Arrests almost ceased during the spring of 1862, when the North was confident of soon winning the war. But the reverses of summer, the mushrooming of Copperhead sentiment, and the resistance to the militia draft in the fall of 1862 produced a new wave of military arrests. Lincoln's September 24 proclamation suspending *habeas corpus* was aimed mainly at this draft resistance.

Altogether during the war, Union authorities arrested at least 15,000 civilians. Was this an excessive repression of civil liberties? Many contemporaries certainly thought so. They did not question the arrest of enemy agents and saboteurs or the military trials of guerrillas and spies in active war zones. (Some critics even sanctioned the military arrest and trial of draft evaders and of persons encouraging desertion or draft resistance, although some of these activities occurred in Northern states where the civil courts were functioning.) But they condemned the arbitrary arrest of editors, public officials, and other persons whose only crime was to write or speak against the administration's war policies or in favor of peace. Some of those arrested were victims of wild rumors of conspiracy that became an inevitable part of war psychology. Some were imprisoned for months without any charges having been brought against them. All of this seems to confirm that the administration's record on civil liberties was a bad one.

Arrests Not Political or Arbitrary

It was not difficult to see why arrests under Secretary of State William H. Seward caused so few political problems for the Lincoln administration. Few of them had anything to do with conventional politics. The discovery that many of the prisoners were citizens of the Confederacy, blockade-runners, foreign nationals, returning Southern sea captains, and the like explained the lack of violent political reaction. Such people were not voters in the North.

Research in the National Archives to discover the sources of F.C. Ainsworth's influential 13,535 figure for arrests in the period after February 1862 (when War Secretary Edwin M. Stanton was in control of internal security) began to uncover another problem with older interpretations. A letter about a civilian arrested by the military in New Mexico territory in 1861 provided an early clue. After all, the

Yet there was often a thin line between verbal antiwar activities and those that were obviously treasonable. Was an inflammatory speech urging recruits to refuse to fight an "abolitionist war" an exercise of free speech, or was it aiding and abetting the enemy? Lincoln stated the question graphically: "Must I shoot a simple-minded soldier boy who deserts, while I must not touch a hair of a wily agitator who induces him to desert? . . . I think that in such a case, to silence the agitator, and save the boy, is not only constitutional, but, withal, a great mercy." The President insisted that in a time of grave emergency it was better to arrest too many than too few. "Under cover of 'Liberty of speech,' 'Liberty of the press' and *'Habeas Corpus,'*" he wrote, the Rebels "hoped to keep on foot amongst us a most efficient corps of spies, informers, suppliers, and aiders and abettors of their cause." The civil courts were too slow to

president had not suspended the writ of habeas corpus in New Mexico. This arrest did not have anything to do with the suspension of the writ.

A majority of the arrests would have occurred whether the writ was suspended or not. They were caused by the mere incidents or friction of war, which produced refugees, informers, guides, Confederate defectors, carriers of contraband goods, and other such persons as came between or in the wake of large armies. They may have been civilians, but their political views were irrelevant, even perverse—some were black men and others came into Union lines for the purpose of declaring their loyalty to the U.S. rather than to the Confederacy.

Such prisoners were hardly "political"; nor did their arrests seem "arbitrary."

Mark E. Neely, Jr., *The Fate of Liberty: Abraham Lincoln and Civil Liberties.* New York: Oxford University Press, 1991.

handle these cases in the emergency; and if released on writs of *habeas corpus* to await trial, these persons would continue their treasonable activities. The purpose of military arrests was preventive, not punitive. Men were detained so they could not aid the rebellion; they were released without trial sooner or later, more sooner than later, when the danger had passed. These were strong measures, Lincoln admitted, unconstitutional in times of peace but constitutional "in cases of rebellion or invasion." "I can no more be persuaded," wrote Lincoln in one of his homely but effective metaphors, "that the government can constitutionally take no strong measure in time of rebellion, because it can be shown that the same could not be lawfully taken in time of peace, than I can be persuaded that a particular drug is not good medicine for a sick man, because it can be shown to not be good food for a well one."[2]

Repression Was Historically Mild

One of the most thorough students of wartime civil liberties defends the Lincoln administration. Most prisoners, he found, were treated well during their confinement. Most were in prison "for good reason." Most were released after relatively short detentions unless convicted for actual crimes such as espionage or treason. When military commissions tried civilians, it was usually for a military crime committed in a war zone. . . . The overwhelming majority of the 15,000 arrests occurred in the occupied South or in the border states that because of guerrilla activity and espionage were really part of the war zone. "Considering the imperative demands of the emergency, a fair amount of restraint was shown in the making of arrests. . . . The Government smarted under great abuse without passing an Espionage Act or a Sedition Law. Freedom of speech was preserved to the point of permitting the most disloyal utterances."[3] Although troops patrolled the polls in border states to exclude voters who had not taken an oath of allegiance, free elections took place throughout the war, administration candidates often suffered defeat, and for a time in 1864 it appeared that Lincoln himself would not be reelected. Compared with the draconian enforcement of espionage and sedition laws in World War I and the internment of Japanese Americans during World War II, the infringement of civil liberties during the much greater internal crisis of 1861–1865 seems mild indeed.

Notes

1. Roy P. Basler (ed.), *The Collected Works of Abraham Lincoln*, 9 vols. (New Brunswick, N.J., 1953–1955), V, 436–37.

2. *Ibid.*, VI, 263, 266–67.

3. James G. Randall, *Constitutional Problems Under Lincoln*, rev. ed. (Urbana, Ill., 1951), chaps. 6–8, 19–20; quotations from pp. 154, 155, 520.

THE GREAT
EMANCIPATOR

The Emancipation Proclamation Freed the Slaves

John Hope Franklin

Lincoln issued the preliminary Emancipation Proclamation on September 22, 1862, after the Union victory at Antietam. The Proclamation proposed to free slaves in Confederate states but not those in territories that remained loyal to the Union. The president hoped that freeing the slaves in Confederate territory would encourage them to join with the Union army and thereby improve the Union's chances of victory against the South. John Hope Franklin writes that, despite its limitations, many slaves and abolitionists praised the Emancipation Proclamation for moving the nation closer to total abolition. In the following excerpt from his book *The Emancipation Proclamation*, Franklin contends that the document gave the war greater moral purpose by changing its aim from saving the Union to freeing the slaves. Because of the dramatic change in public opinion that the Proclamation caused, Franklin believes that slavery could not have survived once the document was issued. Franklin is a professor of history at the University of Chicago.

THE CHARACTER OF THE CIVIL WAR COULD NOT POSSIBLY have been the same after the President issued the Emancipation Proclamation as it had been before January

Excerpts from *The Emancipation Proclamation,* by John Hope Franklin, rev. ed., 1995, pp. 112–18. Copyright © 1963, 1965, 1995 by John Hope Franklin. Reprinted by permission of Harlan Davidson, Inc.

1, 1863. During the first twenty months of the war, no one had been more careful than Lincoln himself to define the war merely as one to save the Union. He did this not only because such a definition greatly simplified the struggle and kept the border states fairly loyal, but also because he deeply felt that this was the only legitimate basis for prosecuting the war. When, therefore, he told [New York *Tribune* editor] Horace Greeley that if he could [he would] save the Union without freeing a single slave he made the clearest possible statement of his fundamental position. And he was holding to this position despite the fact that he had written the first draft of the Emancipation Proclamation at least six weeks before he wrote his reply to Greeley's famous "Prayer of Twenty Millions [in which Greeley criticized his conservative stance on slavery]."

The War Measure

Lincoln saw no contradiction between the contents of his reply to Greeley and the contents of the Emancipation Proclamation. For he had come to the conclusion that in order to save the Union he must emancipate *some* of the slaves. His critics were correct in suggesting that the Proclamation was a rather frantic measure, an act of last resort. By Lincoln's own admission it was, indeed, a desperate act; for the prospects of Union success were not bright. He grabbed at the straw of a questionable victory at Antietam as the occasion for issuing the Preliminary Proclamation. If anything convinced him in late December that he should go through with issuing the final Proclamation, it was the ignominious defeat of the Union forces at Fredericksburg. *Something* needed to be done. Perhaps the Emancipation Proclamation would turn the trick!

The language of the Proclamation revealed no significant modification of the aims of the war. Nothing was clearer than the fact that Lincoln was taking the action under his authority "as Commander-in-Chief of the Army and Navy." The situation that caused him to take the action was that there was an "actual armed rebellion against the authority and government of the United States." He regarded the Emancipation Proclamation, therefore, as "a fit and necessary war measure for suppressing said rebellion." In another place in the Proclamation he called on the military and naval authorities to recognize and maintain the freedom of the slaves. Finally the President declared, in the final paragraph of the Proclamation, that the measure was "warranted by the Constitution upon military necessity." This was, indeed, a war measure, conceived and promulgated to put down the rebellion and save the Union.

Nevertheless, both by what it said and what it did not say, the Proclamation greatly contributed to the significant shift in 1863 in the way the war was regarded. It recognized the right of emancipated slaves to defend their freedom. The precise language was that they should "abstain from all violence, unless in necessary self-defence." It also provided that former slaves could now be received into the armed services. While it was clear that they were to fight to save the Union, the fact remained that since their own fate was tied to that of the Union, they would also be fighting for their own freedom. The Negro who, in December 1862, could salute his own colonel instead of blacking the boots of a Confederate colonel, as he had been doing a year earlier, had a stake in the war that was not difficult to define. However loyal to the Union the Negro troops were—and they numbered some 190,000 by April 1865—one is inclined to believe that they were fighting primarily for freedom for themselves and their brothers in the months that followed the issuance of the Emancipation Proclamation.

Despite the fact that the President laid great stress on the issuance of the Proclamation as a military necessity, he did not entirely overlook the moral and humanitarian significance of the measure. And even in the document itself he gave some indication of his appreciation of this particular dimension that was, in time, to eclipse many other considerations. He said that the emancipation of the slaves was "sincerely believed to be an act of justice." This conception of emancipation could hardly be confined to the slaves in states or parts of states that were in rebellion against the United States on January 1, 1863. It must be recalled, moreover, that in the same sentence that he referred to emancipation as an "act of justice" he invoked "the considerate judgment of mankind and the gracious favor of Almighty God." This raised the Proclamation above the level of just another measure for the effective prosecution of the war. And, in turn, the war became more than a war to save the integrity and independence of the Union. It became also a war to promote the freedom of mankind.

Throughout the previous year the President had held to the view that Negroes should be colonized in some other part of the world. And he advanced this view with great vigor wherever and whenever possible. He pressed the Cabinet and Congress to accept and implement his colonization views, and he urged Negroes to realize that it was best for all concerned that they should leave the United States. It is not without significance that Lincoln omitted from the Emancipation Proclamation any reference to colonization. It seems clear that the President had abandoned hope of gaining support for his scheme or of persuading Negroes to leave the only home they knew. Surely, moreover, it would have been a most incongruous policy as well as an ungracious act to have asked Negroes to perform one of the highest acts of citizenship—fighting for their country—and then invite them to leave. Thus, by inviting Negroes into the armed services and omitting all mention of colonization, the President indicated in the Proclamation that Negroes would enjoy a status that went beyond mere freedom. They were to be free persons, fighting for their *own* country, a country in which they were to be permitted to remain.

The Beginning of the End of Slavery

The impact of the Proclamation on slavery and Negroes was profound. Negroes looked upon it as a document of freedom, and they made no clear distinction between the areas affected by the Proclamation and those not affected by it. One has the feeling that the interest of the contrabands in Washington in seeing whether their home counties were excepted or included in the Proclamation was an academic interest so far as their own freedom was concerned. After all, they had proclaimed their own freedom and had put themselves beyond the force of the slave law or their masters. The celebration of the issuance of the Proclamation by thousands of Negroes in Norfolk illustrates the pervasive influence of the document. President Lincoln had said that Norfolk slaves were not emancipated by his Proclamation. Norfolk Negroes, however, ignored the exception and welcomed the Proclamation as the instrument of their own deliverance.

Slavery, in or out of the Confederacy, could not possibly have survived the Emancipation Proclamation. Slaves themselves, already restive under their yoke and walking off the plantation in many places, were greatly encouraged upon learning that Lincoln wanted them to be free. They proceeded to oblige him. There followed what one authority has called a general strike and another has described as widespread slave disloyalty throughout the Confederacy. Lincoln understood the full implications of the Proclamation. That is one of the reasons why he delayed issuing it as long as he did. Once the power of the government was enlisted on the side of freedom in one place, it could not successfully be restrained from supporting freedom in some other place. It was too fine a distinction to make. Not even the slaveholders in the excepted areas could make it. They knew, therefore, that the Emancipation Proclamation was the beginning of the end of slavery for them. Many of them did not like it, but the realities of the situation clearly indicated what the future had in store for them.

The critics of the Lincoln Administration stepped up their attack after January 1, 1863, because they fully appreciated the fact that the Proclamation changed the character of the war. Orestes A. Brownson, Clement L. Vallandigham, William C. Fowler, Samuel S. Cox, and others insisted that the Proclamation represented a new policy that made impossible any hasty conclusion of the struggle based on a compromise. The President had become the captive of the abolitionists who had persuaded him to change the war aims from preservation of the Union to abolition of slavery. Some of them, such as Vallandigham, were proslavery and openly defended the "peculiar institution" against what they called unconstitutional interference. Others, such as Fowler, felt that the question of slavery was extraneous and the introduction of emancipation into the picture was an act so loathesome as to be virtually criminal. All agreed that the Proclamation transformed the war into something to which they were even more bitterly opposed than they had been to the war to save the Union.

If the abolitionists had pined ascendancy in the councils of the President, they were not altogether satisfied with the results of their influence. For months on end, they had been imploring the President to abolish slavery. "Thaddeus Stevens, Charles Sumner, and Henry Wilson simply haunt me with their importunities for a Proclamation of Emancipation," Lincoln complained to a friend in 1862. Outright emancipation of all the slaves, without compensation or colonization and without apologies for it as a military necessity, was what the abolitionists wanted. "Patch up a compromise now," warned Thaddeus Stevens, "leaving this germ of evil and it will soon again overrun the whole South, even if you free three fourths of the slaves. Your peace would be a curse. You would have expended countless treasures and untold lives in vain." Many abolitionists agreed with Stevens, when he said, in early September

1862, that no one in the government seemed to have the moral courage to take the necessary steps to abolish slavery.

In the light of the demands they had been making, the language of the Emancipation Proclamation could hardly have been the source of unrestrained joy on the part of the abolitionists. The Proclamation did not represent the spirit of "no compromise" that had characterized their stand for a generation. There was no emancipation in the border states, with which the abolitionists had so little patience. Parts of states that were under Union control were excepted, much to the dismay of the abolitionists, whose view was ably set forth by [Salmon P.] Chase. Obviously, the President was not completely under their sway, despite the claims of numerous critics of the Administration. For the most part, the Proclamation represented Lincoln's views. It was in no sense the result of abolitionist dictation.

Toward Liberty for All

And yet, when the Proclamation finally came, the abolitionists displayed a remarkable capacity for accommodating themselves to what was, from their point of view, an obvious compromise. Some of them took credit for the begrudging concessions that the compromise represented. They were wrung, Wendell Phillips told a Boston audience, "from reluctant leaders by the determined heart of the masses." A few weeks later he said to a group of New Yorkers, "Possess your souls in patience, not as having already attained, not as if we were already perfect, but because the whole nation, as one man, has for more than a year set its face Zionward [toward Utopia]. Ever since September 22nd of last year, the nation has turned its face Zionward, and ever since Ambrose E. Burnside drew his sword in Virginia, we have moved toward that point. . . . We have found at last the method, and we are in earnest."

Other abolitionists had even fewer reservations. Thaddeus Stevens praised Lincoln's Proclamation. It contained "precisely the principles which I had advocated," he told his Pennsylvania constituents. For thirty years abolitionist William Lloyd Garrison had never been known to make concessions as far as slavery was concerned. Yet, he declared the Emancipation Proclamation to be a measure that should take its place along with the Declaration of Independence as one of the nation's truly important historic documents. Frederick Douglass, the leading Negro abolitionist, said that the Proclamation changed everything. "It gave a new direction to the councils of the Cabinet, and to the conduct of the national arms." Douglass realized that the Proclamation did not extend liberty throughout the land, as the abolitionists hoped, but he took it "for a little more than it purported, and saw in its spirit a life and power far beyond its letter. Its meaning to me was the entire abolition of slavery," he concluded, "and I saw that its moral power would extend much further."

Radical Republicans in Congress Forced Lincoln to Adopt Emancipation

T. Harry Williams

Lincoln believed that to accomplish his aim of saving the Union, he would need to have the support of a coalition of border state representatives, conservative Democrats, and radical Republicans. To maintain the coalition, he avoided taking a radical stance on the issue of emancipation. As the war went on, however, Lincoln discovered that such a varied coalition could not be maintained. As radical abolitionists pushed ever harder for the total emancipation of slaves, Democrats and representatives from the border states became increasingly unwilling to cede to their demands.

According to history professor T. Harry Williams, in this excerpt from his book *Lincoln and the Radicals*, Lincoln stubbornly pursued a moderate course of gradual, compensated emancipation long after the tide of public opinion had shifted to support total emancipation. One example of Lincoln's reluctance to accept immediate emancipation was the battle over the Confiscation Act of 1862, which radicals in Congress had proposed as a way to free rebel slaves. Williams argues that when Lincoln threatened to veto the Confiscation Act, the radicals grew furious and grudgingly amended it according to Lincoln's wishes. Soon after, according to Williams, Lincoln realized that he needed the

Excerpts from *Lincoln and the Radicals*, by T. Harry Williams. Copyright © 1941. Reprinted by permission of The University of Wisconsin Press.

radicals' support, and in September 1862, he finally conceded and issued the preliminary Emancipation Proclamation.

———

THE JACOBINS [RADICAL REPUBLICANS] HAD FORCED LINcoln to take the general they wanted [John Pope]—a man who would fight and who believed in the radical war aims. Visions of greater victories haunted their minds. They dreamed of filling all the commands with radical officers, and of proclamations of emancipation issuing on every hand. And at the same time they scored another resounding triumph over the administration by pushing through Congress measures directed at the destruction of slavery. Steadily the Jacobin machine was seizing the control of the Republican Party, and Lincoln's hopes of a nonpartisan coalition faded rapidly. The weeks of July 1862 were spacious days for radicalism.

Worshipping a False God

An obscure Republican congressman from Maine furnished the Jacobins with a slogan to inscribe on their banner as they drove to conquest. Speaking in the House in February, Frederick A. Pike shouted: "Our duty to-day is to tax and fight. Twin brothers of great power; to them in good time shall be added a third; and whether he shall be of executive parentage, or generated in Congress, or spring, like [the Roman goddess of martial prowess] Minerva, full-grown from the head of our Army, I care not. Come he will, and his name shall be Emancipation. And these three—Tax, Fight, and Emancipate—shall be the Trinity of our salvation. In this sign we shall conquer."

Unfortunately for the radicals, Pike's enunciation of the dogma of the Jacobin faith did not move Lincoln. Not only did he refuse to be converted and repent of his sins, but he stubbornly denied the third part of the Trinity. To the disgust of the radicals he still persisted in worshipping a false god—his policy of a conservative coalition party with but one purpose, the restoration of the Union. He did take one step toward the radical altar, but it was a timid one; and the Jacobins, who demanded an enthusiastic convert or none, repulsed him. Lincoln had always been an advocate of gradual, compensated emancipation, to be accomplished by the only method he considered constitutional—through voluntary action by the states in which slavery existed. Now on March 6 he proposed such a scheme to Congress, largely for the purpose of conciliating the rising antislavery spirit which the radicals were whipping up in the country. Stressing that gradual emancipation was "better for all," he recommended that the government cooperate with any state wishing to free its slaves by providing "pecuniary aid"—in other words, compensation.

Congress passed a bill embodying Lincoln's ideas. But the measure failed to achieve any practical results, primarily because the loyal Border States in which Lincoln hoped to start the process were opposed to any federal interference with their domestic institutions. Nor did the president win over the Jacobins; they were bitterly contemptuous of his scheme. . . .

The Confiscation Act

Although the Jacobins were pleased to hack away the secondary appendages of slavery [by passing bills to abolish slavery in the District of Columbia and in the territories], such victories only magnified their great fundamental purpose—to bring about the emancipation of all the slaves in the Southern states. In July, when [Union general George B.] McClellan had stumbled back from Richmond and the nation was momentarily appalled by his defeat, the radical chiefs thought they saw a chance to accomplish their objective under the guise of military necessity. [Senator Charles] Sumner went to Lincoln immediately, urging a proclamation of emancipation on the Fourth of July to "make the day more sacred and historic than ever." Secretary of State William H. Seward noted apprehensively, in a letter to Charles Francis Adams in London, that the radicals were "demanding an edict of universal emancipation" as a war measure. Hamilton Fish of New York, later to be a great secretary of state under Ulysseus S. Grant, complained to William Pitt Fessenden that the government was "being destroyed by War, without making War"; if the administration would not adopt an antislavery policy, Fish was for peace terms rather than that the country should "spend more treasure and more blood" in a war without a purpose. Enthusiastically Horace Greeley cried in the New York *Tribune* that emancipation by weakening the Confederacy would insure a speedy, overwhelming triumph for the Union. But Lincoln turned his usual irritating deaf ear to the eager radicals. He told Sumner that an edict of freedom would drive three more border slave states to secede,

The Howling Abolition Faction

[Lincoln] very pointedly and properly asked, . . . "What good would a proclamation of emancipation from me do, especially as we now stand? Would my word free the slaves when I cannot even enforce the constitution in the rebel States? Is there a single court, or magistrate, or individual, that would be influenced by it there? And what reason is there to think it would have any greater effect upon the slaves than the late act of Congress (Confiscation), which I approved, and which offers protection and freedom to the slaves of rebel masters who come within our lines? And suppose they could be induced by a proclamation of freedom from me to throw themselves upon us, what should we do with them? How can we feed and care for such a multitude? General Butler wrote me a few days since that he was issu-

and stir up such dissatisfaction in the army "that half the officers would fling down their arms." General James S. Wadsworth, after talking to the president, gloomily reported to Greeley's capital correspondent, Adams S. Hill, that conservatism still dominated the White House. "He says that the President is not with us; has no Anti-slavery instincts," the correspondent informed the home office. "W. believes that if emancipation comes at all it will be from the rebels, or in consequence of their protracting the war."

But the bosses of the Jacobin machine were of no mind to wait on the future. With public opinion ready to accept emancipation, they were determined to jam it down the administration's throat if necessary. Ready at hand they possessed the weapon to accomplish their design—Senator Lyman Trumbull's confiscation bill, introduced in the previous December and hanging fire ever since. In briefest essence, this was a measure which would free the slaves of every person in rebellion against the government and of

---

ing more rations to the slaves who have rushed to him than to all the white troops under his command. They eat, and that is all; though it is true that General Butler is feeding the whites also by the thousands; for it nearly amounts to a famine there." These remarks of President Lincoln clearly show that he has no faith in the miracles which [the abolitionists] so eloquently assured him would finish up this rebellion with a proclamation of emancipation.

But to silence the clamors of our shrieking and howling abolition faction, and to put them to the test of their promises, including a new batch of nine hundred thousand volunteers for the war, President Lincoln has issued his proclamation of emancipation.

"The President's Emancipation Anti-Slavery Proclamation—The Pope's Bull Against the Comet," *New York Herald*. *Abraham Lincoln: A Press Portrait*, ed. Herbert Mitgang. Chicago: Quandrangle Books, 1971.

any person who aided or abetted the rebellion. Its provisions were sweeping enough to satisfy the most advanced Jacobin, and it brought emancipation in the form desired by the radical leaders—by action of Congress instead of the president. From the beginning Jacobins like Thaddeus Stevens had contended that according to the Constitution Congress alone and not the executive could assume dictatorial war powers. It was for Congress to say how the war should be conducted and for what purpose. The radicals wanted emancipation to come from Congress because this would establish a precedent for legislative supremacy over the whole prosecution of the war. Only when they felt uncertain about their control of Congress did the radicals urge emancipation by presidential edict. In July they judged they had the necessary control.

The Confiscation Act was debated at great and sometimes boring length from March until its final passage on July 17. The radical faction backed it solidly, but it met stern opposition from many of the conservative Republicans who condemned the more extreme provisions as unconstitutional. Benjamin Wade, speaking with authority as chairman of the War Committee, championed the bill, although he did not consider it stringent enough. "I would make it stronger if I could," he shouted. "When I have brought a traitor who is seeking my life and my property to terms, and when I become bankrupt in my endeavors to put him down . . . , I have no scruples about the property of his that shall be taken to indemnify me." The Jacobins frankly proclaimed a determination to scourge the South among their reasons for supporting confiscation. Michigan's Jacob Howard said in the Senate that one of the objects of the bill was "punishment, punishment of the most wanton crime ever committed since he who took the thirty pieces of silver betrayed his Lord and Master." Henry Wilson declared that the Republican Party had a solemn duty "to lay low in the dust under our feet, so that iron heels will rest upon it, this great rebel, this giant criminal, this guilty murderer, that is warring upon the existence of the country." When the conservatives tried to maintain that emancipation was a matter for Lincoln to decide, Wade arose with an angry outburst: "The President cannot lay down and fix the principles upon which a war shall be conducted. . . . It is for Congress to lay down the rules and regulations by which the Executive shall be governed in conducting a war."

The President's Veto

By the middle of July it was apparent to all observers of capital politics that the Jacobin machine, despite conservatives and Democrats, would force the Confiscation Act through to passage. Then Lincoln, who had kept out of the fight to this point, quietly let it be known that he would veto the measure in its present form. This information, noised around Congress by administration lieutenants, threw the radicals into sputtering and impotent rage. With Congress ready to adjourn there was no time to pass the measure over a veto. Just as they were about to taste the heady brew of victory, Lincoln threatened to dash the cup away. "If he does there will be an end of him," grimly wrote Henry Cooke, whose Washington office of the great banking house was a favorite rendezvous for the Jacobin politicos. At this critical point Fessenden, entirely on his own initiative, took it upon himself to go to Lincoln to find out the president's objections to the bill. He found Lincoln far from enthusiastic about the entire measure, but willing to accept it if two clauses were eliminated: one which would confiscate the slave property of persons who had committed treason before the passage of the act, and another which would work a forfeiture of the real estate of the offender beyond his natural life. To the Jacobins the retroactive provision and permanent forfeiture were the soul of the act, and they were wild with anger at the president's obduracy. . . .

The Jacobins might rage but they had to surrender if they wanted their bill. So on July 17, when the measure came up for final approval, they reluctantly and sullenly attached to it an explanatory resolution removing the clauses to which Lincoln had objected. With this change the president signed the act. . . .

The despair that enveloped the radicals was not justified by the facts of the situation. In the Confiscation Act, even after it was modified, they had scored a substantial triumph and had taken a long step toward emancipation. Going into effect as soon as it was passed, the bill declared free the slaves of every person found guilty of treason after its passage, and of all persons who in any way aided or supported the rebellion. If this provision could have been enforced, it would have struck the shackles from practically every slave in the South. On paper the act set free more slaves than did Lincoln's later Emancipation Proclamation, which was also a paper edict so far as immediate concrete results were concerned. . . .

Yielding to Pressure

Abraham Lincoln caught the significance of events in those hot July days when the spirit of radicalism burgeoned in the nation and the Jacobins in Congress wrenched from him the control of the Republican Party. He knew at last that the radicals represented an implacable force which he could not ignore and to which perhaps he must yield. On July 10, while driving to the funeral of War Secretary Edwin M. Stanton's infant son, he confided to Seward and Secretary of the Navy Gideon Welles, who were in the carriage with him, that he had decided to issue a proclamation of freedom. And on the twenty-second he startled the other members of the Cabinet by reading to them the draft of an edict freeing the slaves in the rebellious states. He would have given it to the country immediately, had not Seward argued that the moment was not propitious. Wait for a military victory, he urged, otherwise the proclamation would impress the world as a shriek of despair from an expiring government. Lincoln saw the wisdom of this advice. He put the document aside and looked about for a general who could win him a triumph. At this moment [General] John Pope was shouting that if he had the Army of the Potomac he would march into Richmond.

Other reasons than fear of the Jacobins helped mold Lincoln's decision to free the slaves by executive action. Undoubtedly he had in mind the critical foreign situation: certain European countries were on the verge of extending diplomatic recognition to the Confederacy. In England and France the liberal parties favored the Union cause; they believed the North was fighting the battle of democracy against aristocracy. But they found it difficult to justify their position when the government of the United States proclaimed again and again that its only purpose in waging war was to restore the Union. Lincoln knew that a bold declaration of an antislavery policy would rally the European liberals and inspire them to oppose any friendly gestures by their governments toward the Confederacy. But bulking larger in Lincoln's thoughts than the uncertainties of diplomatic developments were the grave issues of domestic politics. The strongest cornerstone of his program had been the all-parties coalition of Republicans, Democrats, and loyal slaveholders, to fight the war to a conclusion. To hold this discordant conglomeration together it was imperative that he be able to repress the abolitionist instincts of his own party. This Lincoln could not do. Every time the Republicans, the dominant and most numerous element in the combination, moved toward radicalism, the other factions took fright and drew away. And in the summer of 1862 the Republican Party was rapidly going radical. The Confiscation Act, repudiating the purposes of the war as defined in the Crittenden Resolution [which sought to compromise with the South on the issue of slavery in order to restore the Union], smashed Lincoln's plan beyond repair. He had lost the Border States and many of the conservatives. There remained only the Republicans. And while he had hoped to build an inclusive political alliance to sustain his efforts to restore the Union, it was important above all else that he have the support of his own ardent followers. Without their aid he could not preserve the American experiment in government. Nor was he blind to the mounting Jacobinism among the people whose tribune he always considered himself to be. If they demanded that the Union be saved through emancipation, Abraham Lincoln would save it that way.

Lincoln Held a Lifelong Commitment to Emancipation

LaWanda Cox

In the following excerpt from her book *Lincoln and Black Freedom*, LaWanda Cox argues that Lincoln merits the high praise he has received for issuing the Emancipation Proclamation. She claims that Lincoln had always felt a strong repugnance for slavery and possessed a fundamental belief that all men are created equal. Cox maintains that Lincoln pursued a steady course toward emancipation within the constraints of popular sentiment and the Constitutional restraints upon the power of the president. According the author, Lincoln knew that he could not simply abolish slavery because he believed it was wrong, and that explains why the Emancipation Proclamation was written as a dispassionate war measure rather than as an eloquent denunciation of slavery. Furthermore, Lincoln's racial attitudes were progressive, and throughout his life, he treated African-Americans with respect. Cox is professor emerita at Hunter College and the Graduate Center of the City University of New York.

L INCOLN HELD A DEEPLY FELT CONVICTION THAT SLAVERY was morally wrong and should be placed on the road to extinction. In championing a moderate program of denying slavery expansion in the territories rather than

Excerpts from *Lincoln and Black Freedom: A Study in Presidential Leadership*, by LaWanda Cox. Copyright © University of South Carolina, 1981. Used with permission.

joining with abolitionists in calling for a more immediate solution, Lincoln did not disguise his immoderate goal. However unrealistic his expectations, he believed that geographic restriction would ultimately result in slavery's destruction. Yet an incongruity existed in the limits of his policy and the sweep of his moral condemnation. He based the latter upon the authority of the Declaration of Independence, upon its principle that all men (not whites alone) are born equal and entitled to inalienable rights. For Lincoln, limited policy and sweeping principle were morally compatible. During one of the Senate debates with Stephen Douglas in 1858, he advanced the explanation. In defense of the men who had fought for the revolutionary principles of equality and freedom, and then established a government that recognized slavery, he argued that to the extent "a necessity is imposed upon a man, he must submit to it." Slavery existed, and agreement on the Constitution could not have been had without permitting slavery to remain. But necessity did not invalidate the standard raised in the Declaration of Independence:

> So I say in relation to the principle that all men are created equal, let it be as nearly reached as we can.

Removing a Great Wrong

Lincoln's succinct admonition can illuminate his antislavery record as president. It captures a drive, a goal, a fundamental attitude toward men—white or black—consistent with his actions and thus provides a useful perspective from which to examine his role as leader. When war opened possibilities unapproachable in the 1850s, Lincoln's reach was not found wanting. Indeed, there is something breathtaking in his advance from prewar advocacy of restricting slavery's spread to foremost responsibility for slavery's total, immediate, uncompensated destruction by constitutional amendment. The progression represented a positive exercise of leadership. It has often been viewed as a reluctant accommodation to pressures; it can better be understood as a ready response to opportunity. Willing to settle for what was practicable, provided it pointed in the right direction, Lincoln was alert to the expanding potential created by war. Military needs, foreign policy, Radical agitation did not force him upon an alien course but rather helped clear a path toward a long-desired but intractable objective. Having advanced, Lincoln recognized the danger of a forced retreat, a retreat to be forestalled with certainty only by military victory and constitutional amendment. His disclaimer of credit for "the removal of a great wrong" which he attributed to "God alone," though in a sense accurate, for the process of emancipation did not follow his or any man's design, was nonetheless misleading.

After preservation of the Union, the most pressing of the "necessities" to which Lincoln felt compelled to submit as an antislavery man were those imposed by his respect for the Constitution and for government based upon consent. He shared with his generation, Republicans and Democrats alike, a profound attachment to what historian J.G. Randall called "the American people's underlying sense of constitutional government." In imposing radical change upon the South, the Republican majority sought to "keep right" with their heritage of self-government under law, never shed a repugnance for revolutionary means. Historian Alfred H. Kelly and Harold M. Hyman have made this unmistakable; even radical Republicans, to use their words, "'rejected without serious debate the argument for revolutionary legitimacy'" because they were "incurably Constitution-bound." Both Lincoln and his party would bend, if neither would break, allegiance to Constitution and majority consent, but they did not necessarily agree as to what was justifiable.

The constraints under which Lincoln felt he must labor were not always recognized by antislavery men, and this gave rise to charges of irresolute policy and wavering commitment. In striving for consent, he would tailor an argument to fit his hearer. To develop public support or outflank opposition, he would at times conceal his hand or dissemble. And he kept his options open. While such skills added to his effectiveness, they also sowed mistrust and confusion. Similarly misunderstanding arose from his constitutional scruples, which he applied to congressional action as well as his own. Also diminishing the recognition of his leadership was the vanguard position of the Radicals. That he marched behind them should not obscure the fact that Lincoln was well in advance of northern opinion generally and at times in advance of a consensus within his own party. Viewed against his deference to the processes of persuasion and the limitations set by the Constitution, the persistence and boldness of his actions against slavery are striking. . . .

Lincoln's extraordinary effort on behalf of gradual, compensated emancipation is often interpreted as reflecting an overriding concern for moderation, an effort to forestall more radical measures. His actions are more consistent with the view that he sought the largest possible degree of legal security and popular acceptance for an initial move against slavery. There was nothing moderate about emancipation by executive proclamation, upon which he decided in mid-July and acted in September. Lincoln may have preferred gradualism, but he certainly did not insist upon it. Both his July and his December messages sanctioned immediate emancipation. The constitutional amendment he offered in December, which looked to state action over a period extending to 1900, was neither so gradualist nor so compensatory as it appeared. Lincoln's text contained a provision of dramatic potential. Article two would make "forever free" all slaves "who shall enjoy actual freedom by the chances of war, at any time before the end of the rebellion." And only loyal owners would be compensated! . . .

Legal Emancipation

Lincoln's concern for a firm constitutional base for emancipation was consistent, although it did not prevent him from taking action that he recognized might not withstand judicial scrutiny. In defending his revocation in September 1861 of General John C. Frémont's order to free insurgents' slaves in Missouri, Lincoln had implied that congressional authority in the matter was probably more extensive than his own; later he arrived at the conclusion that the war powers of Congress were less ample than those of the commander in chief. In framing a veto of the Confiscation Act of July 1862 [which freed the slaves of Confederates], one made public but never exercised, Lincoln struggled with the problem of how to emancipate legally. He criticized the bill's provisions for freeing the slaves of rebels only to suggest a restatement that would strengthen their legal force: "It is startling to say that congress can free a slave within a state; and yet if it were said the ownership of the slave had first been transferred to the nation, and that congress had then liberated, him, the difficulty would at once vanish."

Until the final Emancipation Proclamation, Lincoln left open an avenue of retreat from executive action, which aroused misgivings among antislavery men. Yet the possibility embodied in the September proclamation that rebel states renew their allegiance before January and thereby escape emancipation, was highly unlikely. Moreover, Lincoln's plea in December for his constitutional amendment [to end slavery] was a clear indication that any southern state returning would be subject to continuing pressure to end slavery. The "hundred days" between [the first and final] proclamations simply strengthened the case Lincoln had been building for his action.

It was characteristic of Lincoln that between his July decision for emancipation and the September proclamation he could keep his intent secret from the public, even appear to deny it. There is the well-known reply to New York *Tribune* editor Horace Greeley of August 22 where he vowed that his paramount object was to save the Union, whether that meant freeing no slave, freeing all slaves, or "freeing some and leaving others alone." In reply to a petition presented on behalf of Chicago Christians of all denominations, Lincoln likened an emancipation proclamation to "the Pope's bull against the comet" and engaged in an hour of discussion raising objections and drawing out counterarguments. Significantly, he raised "no objections against it on legal or constitutional grounds; for, as commander-in-chief of the army and navy, in time of war, I suppose I have a right to take any measure which may best subdue the enemy."

The rub was whether a presidential proclamation of emancipation would "best subdue the enemy." While few except Lincoln's political opponents have questioned the military and foreign policy advantages of the Emancipation Proclamation, another commander in chief no less committed to victory, but not equally moved by the principles of the Declaration of Independence and the evil of slavery, would not necessarily have agreed with Lincoln that the proclamation was his only alternative to "surrendering the Union." Its consequences could not be projected with certainty; its effect upon enlistments, upon the loyalty of border states, upon the morale of fighting men South as well as North held potential dangers for the Union cause. It was a policy, to use Lincoln's own words, "about which hope, and fear, and doubt contended in uncertain conflict." In choosing it "I hoped for greater gain than loss; but of this, I was not entirely confident." Lincoln's concern that the proclamation might hinder rather than advance Union fortunes was quieted only after the event.

Great Restraint in the Wording of the Proclamation

It must have taken great restraint for a man with so eloquent a way with words and so firm a conviction of the wrong of slavery to have fashioned the Emancipation Proclamation in a style that has been likened to that of a bill of lading. An obscure news item [in the *New York Times*] appearing the day before its issuance is worth quoting at length for its explicit and apparently authoritative explanation:

> The President has been strongly pressed to place the Proclamation of Freedom *upon high moral grounds, and to introduce into the instrument unequivocal language testifying to the negroes' right to freedom upon the precise principles expounded by* the Emancipationists of both Old and New England. This claim is resisted, for the reasons that policy requires that the Proclamation be issued as a war measure, and not a measure of morality; and that Law and Justice require that the slaves should be enabled to plead the Proclamation hereafter if necessary to establish judicially their title to freedom. They can do this, the President says, on a proclamation *proceeding as a war measure from the Commander-in-Chief of the Army, but not on one issuing from the bosom of philanthropy.*

Lincoln clearly recognized that as president he had no legal power to act against slavery because it was a moral wrong. That he struggled to subordinate his antislavery convictions to his conception of the powers and duty of the presidency cannot be doubted. To those who opposed his antislavery initiatives, or found them difficult to support, Lincoln was quick to defend his motives as those of commander in chief rather than of moralist by earnestly affirming his "good faith" and arguing the "necessity" of emancipation. At times he seemed to deny any connection between his moral conviction and his official action, but on occasion he presented his case with more subtlety. Most revealing of his justifications was the "little speech" which he made to two influential Kentuckians who in the spring of 1864 came to confer with him about border-state dissatisfaction with his policy. At their request he subsequently put its substance into writing. Lincoln opened with the unqualified statement that he was "naturally antislavery. If slavery is not wrong, nothing is wrong." Yet he understood that the presidency did not confer "upon me an *unrestricted* right to act officially upon this judgment and feeling.... And I aver that, to this day, I have done no official act in *mere* deference to my abstract judgment and feeling on slavery." Lincoln continued with the argument of "indispensable necessity" for emancipation and arming blacks, but at the same time acknowledged as quoted above that he had not been entirely confident of results. In closing he added to what he had said earlier the eloquent passage disclaiming any "compliment to my own sagacity" and attributing to God's will "the removal of a great wrong," to which events were "tending." ...

Lincoln's Personal View of Blacks

Lincoln's personal relations with blacks, as well as the legal stance taken by his administration, indicated his readiness to [end] racial discrimination where it lay within his power to do so. Well attested is his respectful regard for [black abolitionist] Frederick Douglass, and this despite the latter's ambivalent and often sharply critical attitude toward the president. Almost in the same breath with which he criticized Lincoln for the limits of his emancipation policy, Douglass gave testimony of Lincoln's personal lack of deference to the color line: "Perhaps you would like to know how I, a negro, was received at the White House by the President of the United States. Why, precisely as one gentleman would be received by another." Lincoln characterized Douglass as "one of the most meritorious men in America." Lincoln's ease in dealing with blacks, and his complete lack of disdain, would seem to belie the passing reference in 1854 to his own feelings as not admitting the acceptance of freed slaves as social equals. Historian George Fredrickson has speculated that Lincoln felt a strong distaste for the Negro's color and an emotional commitment to whiteness and white supremacy but could control his prejudices because he recognized their irrational character. With so little evidence, and that weighted against racial antipathy, Fredrickson's argument is extremely tenuous. If emotion did indeed contend with logic in Lincoln the president, logic was clearly the victor. One circumspect outburst, however, suggests that the prejudice of whites rather than the presence of blacks taxed Lincoln's capacity for restraint. In the summer of 1864 a telegram from a Pennsylvanian urged his attention to "Equal Rights and Justice to all white men in the United States forever. White men is in class number one and black men is in class number two & must be governed by white men forever." Lincoln drafted a caustic reply, but had it sent over the signature of his secretary:

> I will thank you to inform me, for his [the President's] use, whether you are either a white man or black one, because in either case, you can not be regarded as an entirely impartial judge. It may be that you belong to a third or fourth class of *yellow* or *red* men, in which case the impartiality of your judgment would be more apparent.

Lincoln Believed That Saving the Union and Ending Slavery Were Inseparable Goals

David Livingstone

The U.S. Constitution is based on the principles outlined in the Declaration of Independence, which declares that "all men are created equal." In the following selection, political scientist David Livingstone contends that Abraham Lincoln believed that the fundamental nature of the Union he was trying to save was based on this idea of liberty for all. In consequence, Lincoln believed that in order to save the Union, slavery had to be abolished. Some historians criticized Lincoln for moving too slowly toward emancipation, and have questioned his dedication to equality. However, Livingstone maintains that Lincoln's respect for the Constitution required that he move only as quickly as public opinion would permit, since he was an elected instrument of the people. Livingstone has an M.A. in political science from the University at Alberta, Canada and is completing his Ph.D. in political science at the University of Dallas.

———————————————— ███████ ————————————————

P OLITICAL ANALYSTS HAVE ARGUED THAT PRESIDENT LIN-
coln's Emancipation Proclamation of 1862–63 raised
the aims of the Civil War to a higher moral plane, and his-

Excerpts from "The Emancipation Proclamation, the Declaration of Independence, and the Presidency: Lincoln's Model of Statesmanship," by David Livingstone, *Perspectives on Political Science*, Fall 1999. Reprinted with permission of the Helen Dwight Reid Educational Foundation. Published by Heldref Publications, 1319 Eighteenth St. NW, Washington, DC 20036-1802. Copyright © 1999.

torian James McPherson goes so far as to call the proclamation a "revolutionary" document. By issuing the proclamation, the argument goes, Lincoln effectively served notice to the rebel states that the war was now about saving the Union and about abolishing slavery. Prior to that Lincoln apparently had pursued the merely political objective of saving the Union, a goal that McPherson and others seem to think was unrelated, in Lincoln's mind, to the goal of ending slavery. Contemporary scholars such as McPherson typically do not give Lincoln credit for a long-term political strategy that eventually led to the end of slavery. One often reads, therefore, that Lincoln was forced to emancipate slaves simply because of the deteriorating circumstances of the war or because he was feeling political pressure from Republican abolitionists. Mark Neely suggests that, even as late as 1861, Lincoln had no firm constitutional ideas on the question of emancipation. Thus if the Emancipation Proclamation raised the moral plane of the Civil War, Lincoln had to be either educated or pressured into seeing that higher purpose.

Lincoln's Statesmanship

Following this line of argument, one is tempted to conclude that Lincoln lacked either the vision or the will to attack slavery directly and that he was a reluctant emancipator. Such a view surrenders to the dominant belief that all politicians act only for reasons of power and never for moral reasons—that is, that statesmanship does not exist. To conclude this signifies that scholars do not recognize Lincoln's political prudence, a prudence that harks back to an Aristotelian sense of that term, meaning a faculty for knowing man's proper and highest political end and the means to achieve that end. Lincoln found that highest political end to be expressed by the Declaration of Independence. Although power politics and interest group pressure may explain the actions of most politicians of our day, who substitute public opinion for principles, they do not suffice to explain Lincoln's actions. They cannot therefore, explain the actions of all political people and thus cannot be an adequate or complete account of politics. Such explanations exclude the possibility that some few politicians act for noble reasons.

By examining the Emancipation Proclamation we can understand Lincoln's statesmanship. Lincoln did not follow the prevailing public opinion of his day on the matter of slavery, and he tried to elevate the opinion of Americans on the subject while remaining deferential to the principle of the consent of the governed. Returning to a fuller understanding of Lincoln's statesmanship will return the gratitude that Publius [the pseudonym for Alexander Hamilton, James Madison, and John Jay], in the Federalist Papers, says ought to be paid to the individuals "who had courage and magnanimity enough to serve the people at the peril of their displeasure." It will also return us to an understanding of the presidency more noble than the one we see evidenced today, in both theory and practice. Finally, it will indicate that, for the presidency to assume such an elevated role, the Declaration of Independence must be seen as an essential part of the Constitution, because the Declaration is the highest American expression of the ends of legitimate government.

Inseparable Issues

The Emancipation Proclamation may have raised the moral plane of the Civil War in the eyes of many Americans, but Lincoln had never been under the illusion that the war was about any issue other than the future of slavery in the Union. Moreover, to claim that saving the Union was a mere political goal in comparison with the more principled goal of ending slavery is to claim that Lincoln saw the two issues as separable. Yet Lincoln often said that the principle behind slavery was an unjust principle of rule among men;

it was the "same old serpent which says you work and I eat, you toil and I will enjoy the fruits of it." Clearly, slavery contradicts the principle of legitimate government found in the Declaration of Independence, namely, that all men are created equal. It follows from this principle that all just forms of rule must be based on the consent of the governed. Lincoln constantly returned to the Declaration as both the foundation of the Constitution and the basis on which to attack slavery. When he said he was defending the Union, he meant the Union informed by the principles of the Declaration. Therefore, for Lincoln, to preserve the Union was to attack slavery at its very root.

The Republican Party platform, on which Lincoln was elected to the presidency in 1861, explicitly promised to maintain the principles of the Declaration of Independence. Above all, the platform emphasized the principle of the equality of all men. It also recognized the federal character of the Constitution, within which each state in the Union retains the right to "order and control its own domestic affairs." As for the vast, undeveloped territories to the west that were on the brink of becoming states, the Republicans denied that either Congress or territorial legislatures, or indeed any individual, could give legal existence to slavery in any "territory" of the United States. Lincoln's party concluded that the "normal condition of all the territory of the United States is freedom." The slave states were not, therefore, in accord with the "normal condition" of the United States. Slavery was an aberration, inconsistent with the very principles of a nation conceived in liberty. Furthermore, the Republican Party was pledged to do everything possible within the bounds of the Constitution to create a "normal condition" throughout the Union.

In many respects the Republican platform simply condensed and restated arguments Lincoln had voiced in the 1850s slavery debates with Democratic Party leader Stephen Douglas. During the debates Lincoln acknowl-

A Monstrous Injustice

During his bid for a Senate seat in 1854, Lincoln entered into "The Great Debates" with Stephen Douglas, his main contender. Throughout the year, Lincoln responded to charges that Douglas made regarding his stance on the slavery issue. In Lincoln's speech at Peoria, Illinois on October 16, 1854, he explains to Douglas why he disliked the repeal of the Missouri Compromise, which he believed stopped the spread of slavery. In the following excerpt from that speech, Lincoln argues that slavery is incompatible with the doctrines upon which the United States was founded.

The spread of slavery, I can not but hate. I hate it because of the monstrous injustice of slavery itself. I hate it because it deprives our republican example of its just influence in the world—enables the enemies of free institutions, with plausibility, to taunt us as hypocrites—causes the real friends of freedom to doubt our sincerity, and especially because it forces so many really good men amongst ourselves into an open war with the very fundamental principles of civil liberty—criticizing the Declaration of Independence, and insisting that there is no right principle of action but *self-interest.*

Abraham Lincoln, "The Repeal of the Missouri Compromise and the Propriety of Its Restoration: Speech at Peoria, Illinois, In Reply to Senator Douglas, October 16, 1854." *Abraham Lincoln: His Speeches and Writings*, ed. Roy P. Basler. Cleveland, OH: World Publishing Co., 1946.

edged that the Constitution of 1787 provided guarantees for slavery where it existed in the Union. That compromise, he argued, had been necessary to establish the Constitution at all. However, it did not mean that all or even most of the Founding Fathers supported slavery. Thomas Jefferson, for one, knew that slavery was utterly incompatible with the principles of the Declaration. In a speech given in 1857, Lincoln asserted that the authors of the Declaration of Independence were not so naive as to think that all men at the time actually enjoyed their equal rights to life, liberty, and the pursuit of happiness. They meant simply to declare the right, so that the enforcement of it might follow as fast as circumstances would permit. They meant to set up a standard maxim for free society, which should be familiar to all, and revered by all; constantly looked to, constantly labored for, and even though never perfectly attained, constantly approximated, and thereby constantly spreading and deepening its influence, and augmenting the happiness and value of life to all peoples of all colors everywhere. . . .

An Instrument of the People

Lincoln could not have acted any sooner or more forcefully with respect to slavery because the American people would not have permitted it. Had he moved more quickly to emancipate slaves or used unconstitutional means to do so, he would have lost all political support, at the cost of the Union. Lincoln said as early as 1858 that public opinion was of utmost importance in determining how effective a republican government could be in pursuing policies. "In this and like communities," he said, "public sentiment is everything. With public sentiment, nothing can fail; without it nothing can succeed. Consequently he who molds public sentiment, goes deeper than he who enacts statutes or pronounces decisions." Lincoln argued against Stephen Douglas that the real issue behind the repeal of the Missouri Compromise [which established a line below which slavery was permitted, and above which it was prohibited] and the Dred Scott decision [which ruled that slaves were not citizens of the United States] was not understood by the electorate. That issue was the spread of slavery into the new territories. Those who had a stake in the spread of slavery deliberately obscured the issue. Lincoln reentered politics to bring to light the real issue behind Douglas's "popular sovereignty" banner, which could then be judged accordingly. Lincoln's strategy was to bring before the people true facts and true reasoning based on the first principles of the regime. He believed that if shown the facts and the irrefutable reasons that slavery contradicted the Declaration of Independence, the public would eventually put an end to slavery. That could have happened gradually had more of the border states accepted Lincoln's arguments. But the principle of republican government required that they make the decision themselves, and Lincoln never took that responsibility from them. "As we review Lincoln's plan," historian Harry Jaffa writes, "we must be struck by the almost Jeffersonian fundamentalism where with he sought constitutional authority for policies which carried the federal government in a wholly new sphere of legislation; and how, while exercising the leadership of the President of the whole United States, for a national plan, he tried to secure the sanction of the people in the states, acting through state authority, to carry it into effect."

When Lincoln became president he saw that there was no inherent contradiction between his duty to uphold the Constitution and his firm belief that slavery would someday cease to be protected by the Constitution. The Proclamation was not the result of an unjust desire to avoid the issue of emancipation for as long as possible. The political pressure was there for Lincoln to proclaim a much more comprehensive emancipation, but he resisted—not because he did not want to end slavery, but because to do so would set him on the "boundless field of absolutism." Lincoln sought to bring the people to make the right decision for themselves through appropriate and legitimate avenues of self-government. In doing this, he balanced his roles as elected instrument of the people and elected leader of the people.

CHAPTER

4

RECONSTRUCTION

The Price of Conservatism: The Failure of Lincoln's 10 Percent Plan

Avery Craven

As the Union began taking territories in the rebel states, Lincoln and Congress began proposing ways to bring conquered areas back into the Union, a process called Reconstruction. The president devised the 10 Percent Plan, which required that a seceded state obtain an oath of allegiance from 10 percent of the voters before it would be admitted back into the Union. Radicals in Congress criticized Lincoln's plan as too lenient and instead tried to enact the Wade-Davis Bill, which would have required that a majority of voters swear loyalty and that the seceded states' new governments abolish slavery and repudiate secession.

In the following excerpt from his book *Reconstruction: The Ending of the Civil War*, Avery Craven also argues that Lincoln's 10 Percent Plan was too conservative. Craven contends that it did nothing to change the South's thinking on race and class, nor did it provide for the social integration and economic security of the freed slaves. Craven was a well-known American historian who specialized in mid-nineteenth century American history, particularly the antebellum South. He wrote several books on the Civil War, including *The Civil War in the Making* and *Repressible Conflict*.

Excerpts from *Reconstruction: The Ending of the Civil War*, by Avery Craven. Copyright © 1969, Holt, Rinehart and Winston, Inc.

A S THE WAR WAS COMING TO AN END, LINCOLN BEGAN EX-
perimenting with his plan for quick reconstruction.
In southern states where federal troops had established a
firm foothold, he appointed military governors who were
to encourage and organize Union sentiment and bring
loyal governments into being under his 10 percent proposal. In this way he soon had military governors at work in
Tennessee, Arkansas, and Louisiana. He had no final, fixed
program; he was just experimenting. He told his officials
in Louisiana, which was to serve as a test case, to follow the
forms of law as far as convenient, but at all events to get the
expression of loyalty from the largest number of people
possible. The situation was, he said, "so new and unprecedented . . . that no exclusive and inflexible plan can be prescribed as to details and collaterals."

So uncertain was Lincoln of the final course to be followed that he frankly said that if any loyal southern state
wished to follow the Wade-Davis procedure (which he had
pocket-vetoed), he would be "fully satisfied." He evidently
would have one plan for one state, a different plan for another state, as practical circumstances dictated.

Any attempt to echo what was in Lincoln's mind is, of
course, only conjecture. As an astute politician, he may
have realized that his party had been, and probably still
would be, a minority party when the nation resumed a
normal course. By a quick and generous restoration of the
southern states, he may have been aiming at the building
of a southern Republican wing on old Whig foundations.
He may have been only expressing the deep human qualities which were part of a man to whom war had brought
much of sorrow but little of hatred.

The 10 Percent Plan

At any rate, under his 10 percent plan reconstruction in
Louisiana proceeded rapidly. The test oath was adminis-
tered, a convention was called, a constitution was formed

prohibiting slavery, and a governor and United States senators were chosen. Internal affairs were left largely to the people, yet Lincoln suggested to Governor Michael Hahn that the vote be given to qualified Negroes. He noted that only the United States Senate had the right to decide on the admission of the Louisiana senators. This matter was, therefore, referred to the Senate Judiciary Committee. On February 17, 1865 its chairman, Lyman Trumbull, reported a joint resolution: "That the United States do hereby recognize the government of the State of Louisiana as a legitimate government of the said state and entitled to the guarantees and all other rights of a State Government under the Constitution of the United States."

Abolitionist Charles Sumner, who had been demanding the vote for all Negroes, bitterly opposed this resolu-

A Failure in Style and Method

Some commentators ascribe the failure of Lincoln's Reconstruction plan to his conservative views on race and his reluctance to put freed slaves on an equal footing with whites. In the following excerpt from his book The American Civil War, *historian Peter J. Parish agrees that Lincoln's plan failed, but he does not believe that the president was reluctant to grant freed slaves equality. On the contrary, Parish maintains that Lincoln's approach failed because of his style and method.*

In reconstruction as in emancipation also, the hazards and shortcomings of [Lincoln's] experimental, flexible, step-by-step approach steadily became apparent. The danger of a non-committal attitude was that problems which might have been nipped in the bud were allowed to sprout and spread into a thick undergrowth. The danger of disguising one's real objectives was that intentions were easily misinterpreted or misunderstood. Lincoln was certainly not untion and started a filibuster to prevent its adoption. Caught with the necessity of passing an army and navy bill, the Senate yielded and the resolution was set aside. Louisiana would have to wait.

After much confusion and uncertainty, both Tennessee and Arkansas also held conventions and framed constitutions abolishing slavery and repudiating secession. The government of Virginia under Francis Harrison Pierpont was recognized as the legitimate government of that state. With Lincoln's death and with growing resistance in Congress, none of these three states was admitted. Further steps toward reconstruction thus fell to President Andrew Johnson, who came from a state not yet a member of the Union. It should be noted that many who had opposed Lincoln's southern experiments welcomed Johnson's ac-

aware of the need for conditions and guarantees as part of a policy for reconstruction; indeed he was an early protagonist of the view that emancipation must be just such a condition. But the elusiveness and tentativeness of his statements on Negro civil and political rights created profound misgivings about his whole conception of the scope and purpose of reconstruction. Both emancipation and reconstruction on the Lincoln model were more bold and farreaching than they appeared at first sight; but, by their concentration on immediate tasks and individual situations, and their weakness in planning ahead, they failed to provide an adequate foundation and a sturdy framework for the difficult transition of the Negro from slavery to freedom. This was not a failure of heart or will or conscience, but a flaw in a style and method which, in other respects, reaped handsome rewards.

Peter J. Parish, *The American Civil War*. New York: Holmes and Meier, 1975.

cession to the Presidency. They agreed with Indiana Senator George W. Julian that Lincoln's removal "would prove a godsend to the country." They had already met to urge a new cabinet and "a line of policy less conciliatory" than that of Mr. Lincoln, "whose tenderness to the Rebels" and views on reconstruction were as "distasteful as possible."

Lincoln's Conservatism

Historians have generally been reluctant to evaluate Lincoln's reconstruction efforts. They were never brought to a final test, nor did they represent his final thinking on the whole subject. Yet even if we view Lincoln's efforts at reconstruction simply as experiments and not as parts of a well thought-out plan, one simple fact remains: although Lincoln had an efficient army to carry out his program, he failed completely.

Not a single state was brought back into the Union and the bitterness and confusion—both North and South—was increased. Granting Lincoln all the qualities of diplomacy, adroitness, and ability to get along with others, which supposedly would have prevented all that subsequently happened, he still failed to accomplish anything and, at the same time, created enemies in his own party who rejoiced at his death far more than did intelligent southerners.

Why did Lincoln fail so completely and why this angry opposition? The answer seems to lie in the fact that he was too conservative to satisfy the deep but as yet unexpressed demands of his party for "security" and "repentance." In his first message to Congress in December 1861, he had talked of compensation for states that freed their slaves. In his message of December 1, 1862, he had proposed an elaborate plan for ending the war by "delivering" interest-bearing government bonds to any state that would free its slaves, immediately or gradually, up to the first day of January 1900. In each case Lincoln favored colonizing the freed Negroes "at some place, or places, in a climate conge-nial to them." In his much-quoted letter of August 1864 to Charles D. Robinson (written but not sent), Lincoln reaf-firmed his willingness to save the Union "without freeing any slave" if necessary. He then went on to assert that his statement that "reunion and abandonment of slavery would be considered, if offered" was not "saying that noth-ing *else* or *less* would be considered." He closed the letter by commenting that "if Jefferson Davis wishes, for himself, or for the benefit of his friends at the North, to know what I would do if he were to offer peace and re-union, saying nothing about slavery, let him try me."

All this was consistent with Lincoln's declaration that the war was being waged solely for the purpose of saving the Union. He held firmly to the constitutional theory that secession was impossible and that no southern state had ever been out of the Union. It had only been out of its "proper practical relation" to it. He had once said that he "thought the act of secession" was "legally nothing and needs no repealing." He had even been a bit lax about the loyalty oaths, advising one official to have the loyal as well as the disloyal take them because it "did not hurt them" and would swell the aggregate number required for this purpose. So when a reasonable number of the citizens of a state had taken the oath, incorporated into its constitution the fallacy of secession, accepted the abolition of slavery, perhaps given deserving Negroes the franchise and every chance for an education, renounced Confederate debts, and ratified the Thirteenth Amendment [abolishing slav-ery], it should resume its full rights as a state in the Union.

Problems with Lincoln's Approach to Reconstruction

Two things in such a program were lacking. It did not pro-vide adequate punishment for "unrepentant rebels," and it did not offer sufficient guaranty of justice and equality for the Negro. Lincoln had not learned to hate. He most certainly lagged far behind the "radical" element of his party in racial attitudes. He had seemingly accepted conditionally the existing system when he said that if the new state governments "recognized and declared [the freedmen's] permanent freedom, [and] provided for their education," the Executive would not object, "as a temporary arrangement," to "their present condition as a laboring, landless, and homeless class." Furthermore, he had earlier remarked that he did not favor "bringing about in any way the social and political equality of the white and black races . . . qualifying them to hold office, nor to intermarry with the white people. . . ." He had said repeatedly that he believed there were physical differences which would "forever forbid the two races living together on terms of social and political equality."

Lincoln had never in his own state attempted to remove the bar against Negroes voting, holding office, or attending the public schools. He had checked the army officers who had attempted to free the slaves in conquered areas, and, at all times, he had advocated the removal of the Negro, when freed, from the United States. He had never gone further than to say that slavery was morally wrong and that the Negro had a right to eat the bread his labor created. Lincoln would free him from slavery and grant him all the rights of a human being; but beyond that he conceded no plans for a social revolution. He had not even carried out the seizure of Confederate lands that the confiscation acts of 1861–1862 had authorized.

Nor had Lincoln required the southern people either to humiliate themselves or to undergo a complete social and intellectual revolution. He had ignored Congress, and, as the nation's executive, he had attempted to secure a quick return to normalcy in any state where conditions permitted. Lincoln's purpose was to put an end to bloodshed and to resume a national life. In other words, Lincoln had acted like a practical, pragmatic American politician taking what could intelligently be got. On the grounds that it was essential to maintain state identity in reconstruction, he even rejected War Secretary Edwin M. Stanton's proposal to combine Virginia and North Carolina into a single military district. As one critic wrote: "If there was a grievous fault in Mr. Lincoln's administration it was in the fostering of enemies, and the discarding of friends . . . in fattening rebels and starving those who had elevated him to power." This he thought had been carried to the point where rebellion had been made respectable. Lincoln had attempted the impossible. He had tried to run "the Train of Freedom with slavery conductors . . . giving them plenty of money if they would not smash the cars." The only true policy of government, he insisted, was "to the victors belong the control," and no man should be employed unless known "as the enemy of the rebellion." Only then would the nation be entirely safe.

Lincoln's Reconstruction Plan Became Increasingly Radical

Hans L. Trefousse

With the advent of Civil War, questions about how the seceded states would be reintroduced into the Union once they were conquered became uppermost in Lincoln's mind. On one side of the issue were radicals who argued that the seceded states were no longer states but had become territories, wherein slavery could be abolished. On the other side were conservatives who claimed that the seceded states still retained their statehood and all the rights entitled to them by the U.S. Constitution.

Hans L. Trefousse argues in his book *The Radical Republicans*, from which this selection is excerpted, that Lincoln moved increasingly to adopt the radicals' point of view. In his dealings with West Virginia, Missouri, and Louisiana, Lincoln demonstrated how willing he was to concede to the radicals' demands and place radicals into positions of power. Trefousse suggests that Lincoln's plan of reconstruction would have successfully established safeguards for freed slaves, unlike the plan adopted by his successor, Andrew Johnson. Trefousse is Distinguished Professor Emeritus in the Department of History at Brooklyn College in New York and author of several books on the outcome of the Civil War, including *Andrew Johnson: A Biography* and *The Historical Dictionary of Reconstruction*.

Excerpts from *The Radical Republicans: Lincoln's Vanguard for Racial Justice*, by Hans L. Trefousse. Copyright © 1968 by Hans L. Trefousse. Used by permission of Alfred A. Knopf, a division of Random House, Inc.

D URING THE ENTIRE CIVIL WAR, THERE WAS NO MORE CRU-
cial problem testing the relationship between Lincoln and the radicals than reconstruction. How the seceded states were to be brought back into the Union, who was
to restore them, and who was to govern them after their return—all these were questions about which there was little
agreement. Because of the dramatic clashes between the
President and the most advanced wing of his [Republican]
party, many observers have concluded that, had he lived,
Abraham Lincoln would have experienced the same trou-
bles as Andrew Johnson, that his approach to reconstruction was identical with his successor's, and that the radicals
would have broken with the former as completely as they
did with the latter.

Lincoln Versus the Radicals

But is such an interpretation justified? Did Lincoln really
consistently oppose the radicals' proposals for reconstruction or did he manage to cooperate with them? Was his reconstruction policy fixed or was it flexible? And if it was
flexible, to what degree did he allow the radicals to pave the
way for it? To find the answers to these questions, the
wartime policies of both the ultras and the President deserve careful examination.

For a long time the radicals had been pondering the
question of reconstruction. To most of them, the key to the
problem lay in Article IV, Section 4, of the Constitution,
providing that "The United States shall guarantee every
State in this Union a Republican Form of Government." As
early as 1850, one of Secretary of the Treasury Salmon P.
Chase's correspondents pointed out to him that the article
made slavery illegal in all but the original states. Was not
"the peculiar institution" incompatible with Republican
government? In 1858, abolitionist Theodore Parker, apply-
ing the clause even to the original states, made the same
point, and abolitionist Wendell Phillips alerted Senator

Charles Sumner to it. When the Southern states seceded, the article assumed new importance, Unionists in western Virginia invoking it to demand federal assistance. In a pronounced assertion of national power, radical James Hamilton in December, 1860, characterized South Carolina's contemplated action as "State Suicide," a concept which led to the idea that insurrectionary commonwealths reverted to the status of territories. Some observers went further—as early as January, 1861, the notion that rebellious states could be held as "conquered provinces" was bruited about, and several radicals proposed that Yankee emigration into the border states as well as into Texas and Virginia would be the way to secure these areas. For the ultras, emancipation was a *sine qua non* of reconstruction.

Abraham Lincoln's notions of reconstruction were ostensibly different. Much as he detested slavery, at the time of the secession crisis he did not believe that the federal government possessed the right to interfere with the domestic institutions of the states, a point which he stressed in his first inaugural as well as on July 4, 1861, in his message to Congress. "Lest there be some uneasiness in the minds of candid men," he said,

> as to what is to be the course of the government, towards the Southern States, *after* the rebellion shall have been suppressed, the Executive deems it his duty to say, it will be his purpose then, as ever, to be guided by the Constitution, and the laws; and that he probably will have no different understanding of the powers, and duties of the Federal government, relatively to the rights of the States, and the people, under the Constitution, than that expressed in the inaugural address.

But the word "probably" was indicative of his thinking.

To induce the President to alter his views, much preliminary work was needed, a task the radicals readily performed. As chairman of the House Committee on Territories, James M. Ashley had secured a vantage point in matters dealing with the seceded states, and he made the most of it. Introducing in July, 1861, a bill for the establishment of temporary provisional territorial governments in districts conquered from the insurgents, he set the pattern for congressional reconstruction. Although the bill, as well as a similar measure which he advocated in December, was tabled, the broad outlines of the radical program were plain for all to see.

The Seceded States as Conquered Territories

The President did not have to rely on Congress alone for an exposition of radical views. His own Secretary of the Treasury was in full accord with Ashley's position. When in December, 1861, the congressman, accompanied by Senator Benjamin Wade, called on Chase, the secretary became specific. As he recorded the visit in his diary,

> To both of them I gave my views in brief as to the relations of the insurrectionary States to the Union; that no State nor any portion of the people could withdraw from the Union or absolve themselves from allegiance to it; but that when the attempt was made, the State government was placed in hostility to the Federal Government, the State organization was forfeited and it lapsed into the condition of a Territory with which we could do what we pleased; . . . that those States could not properly be considered as States in the Union but must be readmitted from time to time as Congress should provide.

Wade and Ashley expressed their full concurrence.

For the radicals the reduction of the insurgent states to territorial status was so important because they believed that this policy would make it possible for the federal government to abolish slavery in them. To make this point clear, Charles Sumner, on February 11, 1862, introduced eight resolutions expressing his theory that the seceded states, having committed suicide, had forfeited all rights and were therefore territories. To protect the republican form of government, Congress had to take charge. Lest there be any doubt what Congress ought to do in these territories, the senator included resolutions ending slavery in them. But neither the Senate nor the House was as yet willing to accept so advanced a doctrine.

In the meantime, under the pressure of events, the President was already abandoning his conservative stance. After large portions of Tennessee had been conquered, he too sought to secure republican government for the state by appointing Andrew Johnson military governor. Johnson could be expected to be acceptable to the radicals; as the only Southern senator who refused to go with his state, he had

At the Mercy of the Storm

In Lincoln's last public address on April 11, 1865, he spoke of his Reconstruction plan in positive terms. He acknowledged that the experiment to reconstruct Louisiana had not been completely successful, but maintained that the steps already taken there should be built upon, not scrapped. Not everyone who heard his address was in agreement with the president, however. In the following excerpt from the New York World, *published on April 13, 1865, an editorial writer condemned Lincoln's address as a cowardly attempt to subdue the Radicals who were bullying him.*

Mr. Lincoln ought to learn, from the fruits of the Louisiana experiment, how little he has to gain by shirking the questions which it is his duty to meet with a statesmanlike boldness. By a speech anxiously composed to deprecate the wrath of the radicals, he has incurred as strong expressions of their censure, as he could have done by the distinct avow-

given ample proof of his loyalty and was a member of the Committee on the Conduct of the War. Although Lincoln's move did not suit the advanced members of his party—they considered it an executive usurpation of legislative functions—it was nevertheless a good indication of the President's willingness to experiment. That he was not going to adhere strictly to the stand laid carefully down in his first inaugural address he showed by appointing military governors for Arkansas, North Carolina, and Louisiana as well.

The Border States

It was not only in dealing with conquered areas that the President demonstrated how flexible his policy was. The border states, in many ways, became a testing ground for reconstruction policies. Their divided loyalties, the pres-

---

al of a decided policy. He has let the radicals see that he fears them; and has thereby given them fresh encouragement to bully him. It is true that they have a great advantage over him in their predominance in Congress; but Congress cannot meet until December, 1865, unless he calls them together, and, meanwhile, the military *eclat* of our generals will cause the popular current to flow in the President's favor, and float any sound and reasonable policy which he espouses with courage, and supports by weight of his great position. Before December, he may carry forward the work of reconstruction to so advanced a stage that Congress will not dare to face public odium and undo his work. But if he allows himself to be cowed by the radicals, he will drift like a hull without a helm till Congress meets, and then be driven at the mercy of the storm.

New York World, "President Lincoln's Speech of Reconstruction." *Abraham Lincoln: A Press Portrait,* ed. Herbert Mitgang. Chicago: Quadrangle Books, 1971.

ence of slavery, and their fierce factionalism created conditions which forced the President to abandon his earlier caution. They also furnished experience for the radicals who received valuable aid from unconditional Unionists. The interaction between Lincoln and his critics frequently made it possible for both not merely to retain the border's loyalty but eventually to bring about the abolition of slavery as well. . . .

The Missouri Case

The clearest example of the President's willingness to experiment in slave states occurred in Missouri. It was in this border commonwealth that his pragmatic approach in dealing with both radical and more conservative reconstructionists was put to its most severe test. Almost from the very beginning of the secession crisis, Unionists in the state had been divided into moderates and radicals, who, while cooperating against Southern sympathizers, nevertheless bitterly resented one another. The moderates, who soon became virtually indistinguishable from conservatives, were led by Hamilton Gamble, a respected jurist, and William S. Harney, the federal commander in St. Louis; the radicals, by Francis P. Blair and Nathaniel Lyon. Lyon was a zealous red-bearded captain from Connecticut whose military skill contributed significantly to the defeat of the secessionists; Blair, the best-known Republican in Missouri, had excellent connections in Washington, where his brother, Montgomery Blair, was a member of Lincoln's Cabinet. By giving him permission to remove Harney, Lincoln sided with Blair in the first round of the struggle, and for the moment, the radicals were triumphant. But when, shortly afterwards, military commander John C. Frémont took command and began to quarrel with Blair in turn, the situation changed. The former radical leader now made common cause with the moderates who had just inaugurated Gamble governor; Frémont became the hero of the ultras, especially the numerous Germans, and the contentions of the Claybanks and the Charcoals, the new names for the two factions, rent the entire state. Lincoln's revocation of Frémont's emancipation order and his dismissal of the Pathfinder seemed to place him squarely on the Claybank's side.

But the President's action had not been caused by his disapproval of the radicals' aims. Responsible for the safety of the nation, he could not disregard the opposition to Frémont's action, which was especially strong in the border states. When the time was ripe, he himself would go much further.

During the next few years, the controversies in Missouri became chronic. B. Gratz Brown, the editor of the St. Louis *Democrat,* and Charles D. Drake, "a little, fiery debater, intensely earnest and radical," emerged as the spokesmen for the Charcoals, who favored immediate rather than gradual emancipation, opposed Gamble and Blair, and generally believed Lincoln to be their nemesis. While keeping the state in turmoil, they also furnished the leadership for emancipation, Brown himself advocating Missouri's inclusion in the President's proclamation. And they enjoyed close relations with the radicals in Congress.

Lincoln soon found himself sorely tried by the feud. Harassed by both factions, urged to take action against either one or the other, he attempted to bring them together. "I am having a good deal of trouble with Missouri matters . . . ," he wrote on January 5, 1863, to the radical General Samuel R. Curtis.

> One class of friends believe in greater severity, and another in greater leniency, in regard to arrests, banishments, and assessments. As usual in such cases, each question the other's motives. . . . Now, my belief is that Gov. Gamble is an honest and true man, not less so than yourself; that you and he could confer together on this, and other Missouri questions with great advantage to the public; that each knows something which the other

does not, and that, acting together, you could about double your stock of pertinent information. May I not hope that you and he will attempt this?

To Brown, who protested that Curtis was openly in the interests of freedom, while the governor was "secretly in the service of slavery," he wrote that he took no part between his friends in Missouri, of whom he considered the radical leader one. Although he affirmed again and again that he wished to keep out of the quarrel, he incurred the radicals' ire when, in May, he replaced Curtis with John M. Schofield. No matter how much he protested that Schofield had been sent to Missouri to settle the controversy, they were convinced that Lincoln backed their opponents.

The more conservative Unionists, however, were by no means satisfied. In spite of the President's well-known preference for a feasible emancipation policy, they adopted a measure so gradual as to be wholly impracticable. Moreover, Governor Gamble was insulted because Lincoln characterized him as the head of one of the state's factions.

The radicals sought to make the most of their antagonists' predicament. As Drake in August, 1863, informed the President, Gamble did indeed represent nothing but a faction. Lincoln ought to give his support only to loyal people. Brown also appealed to Lincoln to rely on the unconditional emancipationists and dismiss Schofield, and after the population had become incensed because of William Quantrill's raid on Lawrence, Kansas, where the Confederate marauder had committed acts of barbarity, a radical convention met at Jefferson City. Adopting fiery resolutions favoring immediate emancipation, the gathering appointed a delegation to go to Washington and bring about General Schofield's recall.

Lincoln Moves Toward Radicalism

Lincoln dealt skillfully with the delegates. Tactfully pointing out that he considered them true friends of the administration, he reminded them that he still preferred gradual rather than immediate emancipation and that he could not remove Schofield without cause. In a formal reply, which he sent later, he was more explicit. He took notice of their demands that Schofield be replaced with General Benjamin F. Butler, that Governor Gamble's conservative state forces, the Enrolled Militia, be disbanded, and that only properly qualified voters be admitted to the polls. Nevertheless, he concluded that the facts presented to him did not warrant his compliance. "The radicals and conservatives," he wrote,

> each agree with me in all things, and disagree in others. I could wish both to agree with me in all things; for then they would agree with each other, and would be too strong for any foe from any quarter. They, however, chose to do otherwise, and I do not question their right. I shall do what seems to me my duty. I hold whoever commands in Missouri, or elsewhere, responsible to me, and not to either radicals or conservatives. It is my duty to hear all; but at last, I must, within my sphere, judge what to do, and what to forbear.

"God bless Abraham Lincoln," commented the *National Intelligencer.* "He has routed the Jacobins, horse, foot, and dragoons."

The paper was mistaken. The President did not intend to rout the radicals; nor had he done so. As he told the Attorney General after meeting with the Missouri delegation, he really thought "some of them were . . . pretty good men, if they only knew how!" To Schofield, he gave instructions to prevent illegal voting—an order favoring the radicals because it affected largely returned secessionists. And when Governor Gamble demanded federal protection against his extremist opponents, Lincoln refused. "You tell me 'a party has sprung up in Missouri, which openly and loudly proclaims the purpose to overturn the provisional government by violence,'" he wrote.

> Does the party so proclaim, or is it only that some members of the party so proclaim? If I mistake not, the party alluded to recently held a State convention, and adopted resolutions. Did they, therein declare violence against the provisional State government? No party can be justly held responsible for what individual members of it may say or do.

It was clear to him that public opinion in the West was turning toward the Charcoals, a trend which did not particularly alarm him. As he made clear to his secretary John Hay, they were nearer to him than more conservative Republicans.

The fall election resulted in a very narrow moderate victory, and shortly afterwards, the legislature elected two Republican senators. That one of them, B. Gratz Brown, was a radical, and the other, John B. Henderson, a moderate, seemed providential to the President. "I understand, this is one and one," he commented. "If so, it is knocking heads together to some purpose." And the purpose was very clear. As he said to John Hay while talking about the Missouri problem:

> ... these radical men have in them the stuff which must save the State and on which we must mainly rely. They are absolutely uncorrosive by the virus of secession. . . . While the conservatives, in casting about for votes to carry through their plan, are tempted to affiliate with those whose record is not clear. If one side must be crushed out and the other cherished, there could be no doubt which side we would choose as fuller of hope for the future. We would have to side with the radicals.

Although the ultras failed to appreciate him, in December he proved this commitment by finally recalling Schofield. In 1865, the triumphant Charcoals brought about emancipation, an end result made possible by their efforts as well as by the President's willingness to experiment in the re-making of a state. . . .

The Louisiana Case

The President, for the last time, gave every sign of attempt-ing once more [in Louisiana] what he had accomplished so often in the past. Pushed forward by the radicals and held back by the conservatives, he proceeded to take steps at the right time and move in the direction of the extremists. Ex-plaining the Louisiana problem in November to General Stephen A. Hurlbut, he had already stressed his concern for the rights of the freedmen. The state's new constitution, he emphasized, was "better for the poor black man than we have in Illinois." In March, he unhesitatingly signed the bill establishing a Freedmen's Bureau, a measure which the ul-tras had agitated for a long time to assist the powerless in the South. In the spring of 1864, he had privately commu-nicated his ideas on the suffrage to Louisiana Governor Michael Hahn; [in 1865], after the radicals had campaigned for the reform without let-up, he believed the time ripe for endorsing it in public. After receiving a letter from the Chief Justice pleading for the enrollment of loyal citizens without regard to complexion, Lincoln prepared to deliver what proved to be his last public speech. The date was April 11, 1865; Confederate general Robert E. Lee had surren-dered his army, and the war was virtually over. Speaking of reconstruction, the President said:

> The amount of constituency, so to speak, on which the new Louisiana government rests, would be more satis-factory to all, if it contained fifty, thirty, or even twenty thousand, instead of only about twelve thousand, as it does. It is also unsatisfactory to some that the elective franchise is not given to the colored man. I would myself prefer that it were now conferred on the very intelligent, and on those who serve our cause as soldiers. Still the question is not whether the Louisiana government, as it

stands, is quite all that is desirable. The question is, "Will it be wiser to take it as it is, and help to improve it?"

The President was approaching the radicals' position on reconstruction, and after the Cabinet meeting on the next day, Attorney General James Speed told Chase, "He never seemed so near our views." In December, the hostile Count Gurowski had written, "The great shifter, the great political shuffler, Abraham Lincoln, some day or other will turn up a radical." His prediction, if not his assessment, was correct. As long as Lincoln's leadership prevailed, the radicals were able to bring about progress. Without him, things were going to be greatly different.

All of Lincoln's Reconstruction Plans Failed

William B. Hesseltine

As Confederate territories were seized by Union troops during the Civil War, Congress and the president began to devise ways to govern those areas, and eventually, to reintroduce them back into the Union. Lincoln's approach was a conciliatory one, based on the theory that the seceded states had never left the Union and were still entitled to the states' rights granted them in the Constitution. However, Democrats and radical Republicans in Congress had their own approach to the crisis. William B. Hesseltine argues that all of Lincoln's plans met with failure in the face of this opposition. In the following excerpt, taken from his book *Lincoln's Plan of Reconstruction*, Hesseltine maintains that after abandoning one Reconstruction plan after another and conceding to both Democrats and Republicans, Lincoln was left with no plan to reconstruct the nation at the time of his assassination. Hesseltine, a history professor at the University of Wisconsin, has published several books on the Civil War, including *Civil War Prisons: A Study in War Psychology*, and a collection of his essays, *Sections and Politics*.

F OR THE [LAST] EIGHT MONTHS OF ABRAHAM LINCOLN'S life, reconstruction was never far from the first place

Excerpts from *Lincoln's Plan of Reconstruction*, by William B. Hesseltine. Copyright © 1960, The Confederate Publishing Company, Inc.

in his mind. Radical Republicans and critical Democrats alike saw in Lincoln's announced plan and developing program the clear specter of executive usurpation. The Democrats, however, were inclined to remain relatively quiet while Lincoln and the Radicals battled over the issue.

Constitutional Arguments and Moral Appeals

Back of each of the contending positions was an elaborate theory of the nature of the Union and of the war. Each of the protagonists bolstered his contentions and his actions with constitutional rationalization. In the Radical arsenal was the argument advanced by Charles Sumner that the Southern states had committed suicide. By their acts of secession they had ceased to exist as bodies politic, their laws were null and their property no longer protected by legal authority. Into this political vacuum Congress could move, establish law, and determine what kinds of property it would protect. It might also determine which inhabitants of the region might be admitted to political rights. Senator Sumner's theory of political and economic anarchy in the South was unrealistic and too drastic for a people whose nature abhorred a political vacuum. The Massachusetts Senator won few adherents. More appealing was the dogmatic assertion of Thaddeus Stevens, vindictive, acute, and realistic congressman from Pennsylvania. The Southern states, Stevens admitted, had seceded from the Union. They had established a government and had waged a war. The war was bringing victory to Northern arms, and the area of the Southern Confederacy was conquered territory—its lands, its people, and its political future were completely at the disposal of the victor.

Both Stevens and Sumner based their theories on the fact of secession, but Abraham Lincoln rested his case on the doctrine that the Union was perpetual. The Southern states had not seceded. Instead, evil men had seized the governments of the states and had used the apparatus of the state for evil purposes. But the states, the laws, and the property protected by those laws had not ceased to exist. As Lincoln would eventually express it, the states were out of their "proper practical relations" to the national government. The wicked men who had performed the evil act might be punished or forgiven by the President, but the states had not ceased to exist. The President's task was simple: restore them to their proper practical relations.

Bolstering each opposing constitutional argument was a moral appeal. Back of Lincoln's position lay the concepts of humanitarianism and forgiveness and Christian charity. Back of the Radicals were the appeals of human rights and social justice. Lincoln would forgive repentant sinners; the Radicals would wipe out a social evil and establish a greater democracy. In the vocabulary of controversy both antagonists had persuasive arguments, and neither made stark avowal of other objectives. The Democrats, however, could invoke a plague on both houses, accusing the Radicals of predatory designs on Southern property, and accusing Lincoln of ambition to be a dictator.

Yet, whatever the hidden motives of the contenders, there was a strange combination of logic and *non sequitur* in the position of each. No ardent Secessionist would be consistent in objecting to either Sumner's or Stevens' constitutional theories, and had Secessionists reacted on the basis of pure reason, those who had taken up arms against national centralization should have sought an alliance with Radical congressmen who were battling against executive dictatorship. And, had Lincoln sought absolute power, he might have found the enfranchised Negro a more pliable instrument of power than the discordant loyalists and the semi-penitent Confederates whom he was trying to organize. Then, to compound the paradoxes, neither the theory of the perpetual union nor of the conquered provinces carried with it the necessary implication that reconstruction was the exclusive function of either the executive or the legislative branch of the government.

In any case, whatever the clarity of the opposing positions, the issue never came before the great tribunal of the American electorate. After the presidential election of 1864 Lincoln wanted to contend that his plans and proceedings had received a mandate from the people. But the voters had had no opportunity to choose between the two Republican positions. . . .

Filibuster and Concession

The lessons of the 1864 election seemed to stiffen the determination of both Charles Sumner and Abraham Lincoln. To a large extent the [Reconstruction] issue became personal. "Questions of statesmanship press for decision," Sumner told the Englishman John Bright on New Year's Day, 1865. "The President is exerting every force to bring Congress to receive Louisiana under Union general Nathaniel P. Banks government. I do not believe that Louisiana is strong enough in loyalty and freedom for an independent state. . . . I have discussed it with the President and have tried to impress on him the necessity of having no break between him and Congress." And Lincoln was equally disgusted with the Senator. "I can do nothing with Mr. Sumner in these matters," he said in exasperation. "While Mr. Sumner is very cordial with me, he is making his history in an issue with me on this very point."

Making his history though he was, Sumner was willing to concede a little. Privately, he proposed that he would let Louisiana be recognized, if Lincoln would demand Negro suffrage in all the other Rebel states. But the President was adamant. He believed that he had a majority of the Congress behind him. He acquiesced when Congress formally rejected the electoral votes of the Southern states, and he said nothing, when Sumner denounced Governor Francis Pierpont's government of Virginia as nothing more than the common council of Alexandria. General Banks and two newly-elected senators from Louisiana were present in Washington lobbying for admission. Lincoln might well have felt confident in refusing to accept Negro suffrage.

He reckoned, however, without considering Sumner's persistence and his determination to "make his history" on the issue of civil rights and Negro suffrage. Sumner realized that one argument of the President's supporters would be that Louisiana and the other reconstructing states would be needed to ratify the Thirteenth Amendment. On February 11 he attempted to forestall that argument with resolutions contending that, since the Southern states had committed suicide, only three-fourths of the loyal states were needed to adopt the amendment. Further, Sumner proposed that the representation of any state be determined, not by population, but by the number of male voters—a device he hoped would bribe the Southerners to admit Negroes to the polls. But the proposals met no favor. As the New York *Times* pointed out, February 6, 10, 1865, changing the base of representation would cost Massachusetts one House seat and one electoral vote. The paper denounced Sumner's "excessive zeal" for the black men: his plan was "wrong in principle" and "pernicious in effect."

Encouraged by Sumner's lack of support, Illinois Senator Lyman Trumbull brought in a resolution to recognize Louisiana, and on February 25 moved its discussion. Tactically, the resolution was unwise, for Sumner immediately began a filibuster that threatened to hold up all legislation. To his aid came Ben Wade and other extreme Radicals and even Democrat Powell. . . .

The filibuster had its effect. In order to get the ordinary business of Congress completed before the session ended, Lincoln's men withdrew the Louisiana resolution, and the President stood defeated. Democrats joined with moderate Republicans in denouncing Sumner's "outrageous parliamentary tactics" and "factious opposition." As Lincoln saw it, the Radicals who insisted on Negro suffrage were attempting "to change this government from its original form and make it a strong centralized power." But Sumner explained his purpose in a broader frame of reference than a mere political and constitutional one. "Can emancipation be carried out," he asked British radical John Bright, "without using the lands of the slave masters? We must see that the freemen are established on the soil. The great plantations must be broken up and the freedmen must have the pieces." Then, unless the Negroes were given the franchise, "the old enemy will reappear" and "in alliance with the northern democracy, put us all in peril again, postpone the day of tranquillity and menace the national credit by assailing the national debt." In Sumner's mind, social reform and economic reorganization depended on the Negroes controlling the Southern states. "It is said they are as intelligent as the Irish just arrived," he added. "Mr. Lincoln," he sighed, "is slow in accepting truths."

Charity as the Last Resort

Lincoln was indeed slow in accepting Sumner's formulation of truth. Yet, as a pragmatist, he was forced to recognize that each of his plans of reconstruction—the patronage, the governments-in-exile, the military governors, the efforts to organize the Southern Unionists, and the offer of amnesty to a repentant 10 per cent of the Confederates—all had met failure. He had no fanatic devotion to principles drawn from the empyrean, like Senator Sumner; no predatory designs on the property of Southerners like many Radicals; yet, he was unwilling to give up the struggle in the face of repeated failure.

There was, under the circumstances, one course left, if the nation was to be re-made with a minimum of social, economic, and political revolution—an appeal to Northerners and Southerners alike for magnanimity, for repentance and forgiveness. "Let us strive on," he pleaded in his second inaugural a few days after Sumner's filibuster ended,

". . . to bind up the nation's wounds, to secure a just and lasting peace among ourselves and with all nations." It was, perhaps, the most practical appeal he could make. The American people were a Christian people, committed in theory to the practice of charity, to the dogma of the forgiveness of sins. The Parable of the Prodigal Son was a part of the American ethic.

In the five remaining weeks of his life Abraham Lincoln began to formulate yet a new plan of reconstruction. The war was coming to a close and on March 27 Lincoln went to City Point to discuss with General Ulysses S. Grant the plans for the end. To the meeting came General William T. Sherman and Admiral David Porter. With them Lincoln talked about the disposition of the Rebel states. He wanted, he said, to get peace quickly, and the deluded Rebel soldiers back to their homes. He contemplated no harsh measures, no revenge. He implied—with a typical story to illustrate the point—that he would be pleased, if Confederate president Jefferson Davis could escape the country "unbeknownst to me." He implied that Sherman should get the surrender of General Joseph E. Johnston's army on whatever terms possible, and that Sherman should tell North Carolina's Governor Z.B. Vance that, as soon as the Rebel armies laid down their arms, the citizens would be protected in their civil pursuits. Moreover, as Sherman remembered it, Lincoln authorized him to tell Vance that, in order to avoid anarchy, the "state government then in existence" would be recognized as a *de facto* government until Congress might act. Unfortunately, when Sherman met Johnston and embodied his understandings in a convention which amounted to a treaty of peace, Lincoln was dead and the Radical spirit of revenge ruled the cabinet. But before the press, a congressional committee and the public, Sherman maintained that Lincoln's counsels were those of conciliation and forgiveness.

That Sherman correctly understood Lincoln became

evident a week after the meeting at City Point. Hardly had Lincoln got back to Washington than Richmond fell. Lincoln hurried off to the Rebel capital. There he talked to leading Virginians, among them former Supreme Justice John A. Campbell, who far back in the days of the Sumter crisis [when Civil War began], tried to avoid a conflict. Now Judge Campbell hoped to arrange an armistice and negotiate a peace. Lincoln's terms were the simple recognition of the national authority, the acceptance of emancipation, and the discharge of the Rebel armies. Campbell agreed and began to discuss details for implementing the plan. There was the question of Pierpont's government at Alexandria, and there was also a proposal to reassemble the Confederate legislature of Virginia for the purpose of withdrawing Virginia troops in Lee's army. To Major-General Godfrey Weitzel, provost marshal of Richmond, Lincoln issued an order to permit "the gentlemen who have acted as the Legislature of Virginia" to reassemble to "take measures to withdraw the Virginia troops and other support from resistance to the General Government." Should they reassemble, Lincoln ordered, "Give them permission and protection until, if at all, they attempt some action hostile to the United States."

About the meaning of this order and about Lincoln's intentions controversy arose immediately. Campbell assumed that the legislature could act on all matters looking to ending "resistance to the General Government" and could stay in session until it attempted hostile action. Probably, Campbell understood rightly, for Lincoln went back to Washington to discuss the arrangements with his cabinet. He was astonished at the disapproval he met. Secretary of War Edwin M. Stanton and Attorney General Joseph Speed were vehement. To Secretary of Navy Gideon Welles, who was not quite so outspoken, the President attempted an explanation. The Virginia legislature was composed of the prominent and influential men of the counties and he wished them to "come together and turn themselves and their neighbors into good Union men." There must be, said Lincoln, courts, and law and order, or society would be broken up, the disbanded armies turned into robber bands or guerillas. But Welles was not convinced. He too raised the question of Pierpont's government.

Defeated by the lack of support in his own cabinet, Lincoln yielded once more, and for the last time, on a tentative plan of reconstruction. At Stanton's insistence he sent a telegram to Weitzel. Since Lee's armies had now surrendered, there was no reason to reassemble the legislature. Judge Campbell, he explained, had assumed that "I have called the insurgent Legislature of Virginia together, as the rightful Legislature of the State, to settle all differences with the United States. I have done no such thing."

Instead, Lincoln pointed out, he had called them "the gentlemen who have acted as the Legislature" and he had authorized their meeting only to withdraw Virginia's troops from Lee. This, of course, was technically true, but it was much less than the plan Lincoln had presented to the cabinet and argued for with Welles. Campbell, who had discussed the matter with him, thought the President had resorted to a technicality to quibble out of an agreement.

The Collapse of Lincoln's Last Plan

The collapse of this, Lincoln's last plan of reconstruction, left the President without a program. Defeated in succession by the quarrels among Unionists he had hoped to unite, by the failure of Confederates to respond to offers of amnesty, by Radical insistence on programs that contemplated social reform and economic penetration of the South, and even by the revolt of his cabinet, Lincoln made his last public pronouncement on reconstruction with only an attitude to recommend to the victorious Northern people. Returned from Richmond, Lincoln spoke from the White House portico to celebrants who assembled to serenade him. Victory, said the

President, made reconstruction press more closely. "It is fraught with great difficulty." It was, he explained, not like a foreign war in which an "authorized organ" might negotiate a peace. "We must begin with a mold from disorganized and discordant elements." The situation was worse because "we, the loyal people, differ among ourselves as to the mode, manner, and means of reconstruction."

To resolve the difficulty the President—with true pragmatic approach—proposed ignoring the theories of the status of the Southern states. "We all agree that the seceded states are out of their proper practical relation with the Union." The only object of the government was to restore their proper practical relations.

He reviewed the case of Louisiana and his approach was, as it had been from the beginning, a political one. He would have preferred to enfranchise very intelligent Negroes and colored soldiers—but it was beside the point to complain that the Louisiana constitution was not all that might be desired. He would take and improve it rather than dishearten the loyal element. Then, once again, he struck the note that no inflexible plan should be prescribed. He was, he added, considering "some new announcement to the people of the South."

The new plan never came. On the last day of his life Abraham Lincoln discussed reconstruction again with his cabinet, but no new plan came from the meeting. Three weeks later Andrew Johnson announced his plan of reconstruction and in the controversy that followed he alleged that he was carrying out Lincoln's plan. But Johnson's plan bore more resemblance to Henry Winter Davis' bill than to Lincoln's schemes. Perhaps, indeed, Lincoln might have come to that point, but Johnson's inflexible adherence to his own program was far removed from Lincoln's experimental, pragmatic approach to the problem. It is more likely that assassin John Wilkes Booth's bullet found Abraham Lincoln without a plan of reconstruction.

The Reconstruction Myth

Charles Sumner gave his attention to Lincoln's informal remarks on the White House portico. "The President's speech and other things," he remarked, "augur confusion and uncertainty in the future with hot controversy. Alas! Alas!"

It was indeed "Alas!" From the hot controversy that followed there grew the myth of Lincoln's Plan of Reconstruction as a plan which, had he but lived, would have healed the nation's wounds with love and forgiveness. Not a week had passed before the editor of a religious paper, who had been a consistent opponent of the war, struck the new note. "To the general interests of the people, South and North, the prolonged life of Abraham Lincoln has assumed, within the fortnight before his assassination, a value it had lacked up to that period." Grant, said the editor, had treated Lee with magnanimity, "and since President Lincoln had shown the disposition to sustain General Grant, in offering the Confederates terms they could accept without utter degredation, there was a disposition growing among wise and honest men to stand by him and support him." This early formulation of the myth found many an elaboration while the "hot controversy" raged, and long after the Radical plans for remoulding and reconstructing the South, tried for a dozen years, proved as great failures as Lincoln's war-time efforts, the belief grew strong that Lincoln would have brought a different result. In the shock of Lincoln's death men remembered only his last words and forgot that for one or another reason, each of his plans of reconstruction had failed.

Lincoln Was Responsible for the Passage of the Thirteenth Amendment

J.G. Randall and Richard N. Current

The Thirteenth Amendment to the U.S. Constitution, passed by Congress on January 31 and ratified by the states on December 6, 1865, outlawed slavery in the United States. Democrats in Congress had argued that the Amendment was unconstitutional, however, and because the House of Representatives had a Democratic majority, Lincoln knew it would be difficult to obtain enough votes to pass the Amendment.

According to J.G. Randall and Richard N. Current in their book *Lincoln, the President*, Lincoln was the person most responsible for influencing enough House Democrats to change their votes. As a result, the Thirteenth Amendment was passed in 1865, nearly a year earlier than it would have been had Lincoln waited until the House gained a Republican majority. J.G. Randall, often called the greatest Lincoln scholar of all time, died in 1953 before completing *Lincoln, the President*. Historian Richard N. Current finished the book, for which he won the 1956 Bancroft prize.

WHEN THE THIRTY-EIGHTH CONGRESS (1863–65) FIRST met, there seemed little likelihood that a proposal for an antislavery amendment would ever emerge from its sittings. The Republicans, Conservative and Radical, anti-administration and pro-administration, agreed upon the desirability of such a resolution. The Democrats, almost as unanimously, were opposed to it. Its passage would require a two-thirds majority in both chambers. In the Senate the Republicans controlled more than enough votes, but not in the House. When the measure was considered in the first session (1863–64) it met the fate expected of it. When it was reconsidered in the second session (1864–65) it passed, even though the party composition of the House remained essentially unchanged. Its success at that time was due largely to the exertions of the President, acting upon what he considered a mandate from the people in the election of 1864.

Lincoln needed to concern himself little about the action of the Senate, even though rivalries among the Republican leaders seemed at times to jeopardize the party program. Charles Sumner, the anti-slavery veteran, "whose pride of erudition amounted almost to vanity" (in the words of Lincoln's secretaries John Nicolay and John Hay), threatened at first to divide the majority by insisting upon his own wording for the proposed resolution. A month after John B. Henderson, of Missouri, had introduced a resolution, Sumner (February 8, 1864) introduced another one, to the effect that "everywhere within the limits of the United States, and of each State or Territory thereof, all persons are equal before the law, so that no person can hold another as a slave." He desired this proposal referred to the Committee on Slavery, of which he himself was chairman, but finally consented to let it go to the judiciary committee, to which Henderson's resolution already had gone. Lyman Trumbull, chairman of the judiciary committee, reported back a substitute with wording different from that of either Henderson or Sumner, wording adapted from the Northwest Ordinance of 1787. Sumner now tried to reinsert his "equal before the law" phrase, which he had derived from the constitution of revolutionary France. The Senate managed, however, to pass the Trumbull substitute without change: "Neither slavery nor involuntary servitude, except as a punishment for crime whereof the party shall have been duly convicted, shall exist within the United States, or any place subject to their jurisdiction."

Meanwhile Lincoln closely watched the progress of a similar measure in the House, hoping against hope that it might get enough Democratic support to pass. Again and again, consulting with Republican members, he added up the possible votes in its favor, but he could never make a total of two-thirds. After conferring with him, his friend Isaac N. Arnold tested the calculations of Lincoln and the Republicans by introducing a resolution which did not propose an actual amendment but merely declared "that the Constitution should be so amended as to abolish slavery." The vote on this test confirmed Lincoln's apprehensions. When the proposed amendment itself came to a vote (June 15, 1864) only one Democrat supported it with a speech and only four with their ballots. One Republican, James M. Ashley, of Ohio, changed his vote from yea to nay so that, in accordance with the House rules, he could move for a reconsideration of the resolution at the next session of Congress. . . .

Democratic Opposition to the Amendment

While the Democrats reiterated their familiar campaign slogan—"The Constitution as it is and the Union as it was"—they urged most strongly and most repetitiously the argument that the abolition of slavery was outside the scope of the Constitution altogether, that an antislavery amendment would be itself unconstitutional. Senator Saulsbury conceded that all the states, when they made the Constitution, could have prohibited slavery in it. He maintained, however, that after all the states had signed the "contract," a mere three-fourths of them could not alter it in such a way as to destroy a domestic institution that antedated the contract. Representative Pendleton, of Ohio, the Democratic vice-presidential candidate in 1864, put the matter this way: "neither three-fourths of the States, nor all the States save one, can abolish slavery in that dissenting State; because it lies within the domain reserved entirely to each State for itself, and upon it the other States cannot enter." Representative John Pruyn, of New York, added: "The Constitution would never have been ratified had it been supposed by the States that, under the power to amend, their reserved rights might one by one be swept away. This is the first time in our history in which an attempt of this kind has been made, and should it be successful it will . . . be an alarming invasion of the principles of the Constitution." Pruyn went on to say that the disposition of slavery ought to be left to the separate states, or else there ought to be passed "a supplementary article to the Constitution, not as an amendment, but as the grant of a new power based on the consent *of all the States, as the Constitution itself is.*"

That such objections and counterproposals made sense to their authors is understandable, perhaps, when one remembers that the Constitution had not been amended for some sixty years, not since the Twelfth Amendment was proposed in 1803 and ratified in 1804, and that the proposed Thirteenth Amendment was different in a significant respect from any of the preceding twelve. All the others had dealt with "constitutional" matters in a strict sense, that is, with governmental powers and functions. The new amendment would be the first to effect a sweeping social reform by means of the amending process. Yet the objecting Democrats, if they truly had been motivated by constitutional considerations, might have concluded that such an amendment dealt as properly with "constitutional" matters as any article of the bill of rights, concerned as it was with the great subject of human freedom. They might also have reflected that the reserved rights of the states, for which Pruyn and others of them were so solicitous, were guaranteed not in the original text of the Constitution but in one of the amendments, the Tenth. They were on weak ground in making any distinction between the Constitution *and the amendments;* they would have been on better ground if they had thought of the Constitution *as amended.* And they should have recognized that (at least after 1808) the Constitution contained no limitations, expressed or implied, on its own amendability.

These are not merely the reflections of a later generation of historians and political scientists. That the Constitution could be amended freely, if the appropriate procedures were followed, was the common-sense view of that time. "After all," observed a Washington newspaper in January, 1865, "the Constitution is but the legally expressed will of the people, susceptible of amendment whenever they choose to exercise the power." As recently as 1861, less than six weeks before the firing on Fort Sumter, Democratic as well as Republican politicians had given indisputable evidence of the general understanding that the Constitution could be amended for any purpose, even for the purpose of abolishing slavery within the states. By a two-thirds vote in the Senate and the House, they proposed for ratification by the states a thirteenth amendment which provided: "No amendment shall be made to the Constitution which will authorize or give to Congress the power to abolish or interfere within any State with the domestic institutions thereof, including that of persons held to labor or service by the laws of said State." If the Senators and Congressmen had not thought that the Constitution, lacking this proposed amendment, could have been amended so as to abolish slavery, there would have been no point in undertaking to add the amendment. Since the amendment failed of adoption, the Constitution remained as before, with no limit on the ways in which it might be amended. And even if that amendment had been adopted, it of course could have been repealed by another one.

The Voice of the People

The question was not to be decided by the mere oratory of congressmen but by persuasions of a more powerful kind, by the voice of the people as expressed in the election of 1864 and by the President's efforts to see the popular mandate promptly carried out.

Lincoln had done all he could to make the antislavery amendment a campaign issue. From the outset he intended to run on a platform favoring the proposition. In June of 1864, while the proposition was still before the House of Representatives, he called to the Executive Mansion the chairman of the National Republican Committee, Senator E.D. Morgan, and gave him instructions for his speech opening the Baltimore convention. "Senator Morgan," he is reported to have said, "I want you to mention in your speech when you call the convention to order, as its key note, and to put into the platform as the key-stone, the amendment of the Constitution abolishing and prohibiting slavery forever." At Baltimore Senator Morgan did as the President wished him to do, and the delegates responded in adopting the third plank of the party platform, which stated the prevailing Republican view that slavery was the cause of the rebellion and added that the President's proclamations had aimed "a death blow at this gigantic evil" but that a constitutional amendment was necessary to "terminate and forever prohibit" it. In his statements which were used during the ensuing campaign, Lincoln stressed the indispensability of an antislavery policy as a means of winning the war. On this point, rather than the issue of Union or of peace, he differed most sharply with the rival candidate, George B. McClellan.

When Lincoln was overwhelmingly re-elected, he therefore was justified in feeling that his antislavery program had the sanction of the popular will. When, along with him, so many Republican candidates for Congress also were elected that the party would control more than the needed two-thirds majority in the next House of Representatives, he could look forward confidently to the ultimate conversion of the popular will into a constitutional amendment. But the newly elected Congress, the Thirty-Ninth, would not meet in the usual course of events for over a year, that is, not until December, 1865. The President could call a special session of the new Congress to meet at any time after his own re-inauguration on March 4, and he was prepared to do so if the old Congress, the Thirty-Eighth, should fail to act at its last regular session (1864–65). This Congress contained, in the House, the same sizeable minority of Democrats who previously had blocked the passage of the resolution which the Senate had passed. Many of these Democrats now were lame ducks. Lincoln was eager to get the work done, and he counted on enough lame-duck support to get it done before he finished his first term. He stated his views on the subject in his message to the Thirty-Eighth Congress when it met for its final session in December, 1864:

"At the last session of Congress a proposed amendment of the Constitution abolishing slavery throughout the United States, passed the Senate, but failed for lack of the requisite two-thirds vote in the House of Representatives. Although the present is the same Congress, and nearly the same members, and without questioning the wisdom or patriotism of those who stood in opposition, I venture to recommend the reconsideration and passage of the measure at the present session. Of course the abstract question is not changed; but an intervening election shows, almost certainly, that the next Congress will pass the measure if this does not. Hence there is only a question of *time* as to when the proposed amendment will go to the States for their action. And as it is to so go, at all events, may we not agree that the sooner the better? It is not claimed that the election has imposed a duty on members to change their views or their votes, any further than, as an additional element to be considered, their judgment may be affected by it. It is the voice of the people now, for the first time, heard upon the question. In a great national crisis, like ours, unanimity of action among those seeking a common end is very desirable—almost indispensable. And yet no approach to such unanimity is attainable, unless some deference shall be paid to the will of the majority, simply because it is the will of the majority. In this case the common end is the maintenance of the Union; and, among the means to secure that end, such will, through the election, is most clearly declared in favor of such constitutional amendment."

Winning Over the Opposition

Here the President was appealing to the Democratic members of the current Congress, and especially to the numerous lame ducks among them. Other Republicans besides the President were thinking of the possibility of winning over some of the opposition and thus passing the proposal soon, during the winter of 1864–65. "The majority against it in the House was I think *eleven*," a correspondent advised Senator Sumner, "& in view of the feeling of the people, as evidenced by the Presidential vote, I think that a sufficient number of Democrats might be brought over without difficulty to carry it thro at once without waiting for the new Congress." Lincoln did not leave it to his party leaders in Congress to persuade these Democrats to change their votes. He invited a number of them individually to the White House for informal interviews in January, 1865.

One of those he interviewed was James S. Rollins, a

representative from the strongest slave district in Missouri and himself one of the largest slaveowners in his county, who had voted against the amendment in the previous session but who had not been re-elected to Congress. Lincoln said to him (as Rollins afterward reported the conversation): "You and I were old whigs, both of us followers of that great statesman, Henry Clay, and I tell you I never had an opinion upon the subject of slavery in my life that I did not get from him. I am very anxious that the war should be brought to a close at the earliest possible date, and I don't believe this can be accomplished as long as those fellows down South can rely upon the border states to help them; but if the members from the border states would unite, at least enough of them to pass the thirteenth amendment to the Constitution, they would soon see that they could not expect much help from that quarter, and be willing to give up their opposition and quit their war upon the government; this is my chief hope and main reliance to bring the war to a speedy close, and I have sent for you as an old whig friend to come and see me, that I might make an appeal to you to vote for this amendment." Rollins replied that he already had made up his mind to vote for it. Lincoln then asked him to see and talk with other members of the Missouri delegation, and Rollins cheerfully agreed to do so.

Possibly, in talking with some of the Democratic holdovers in the House, Lincoln used the more substantial argument of patronage. At least one of the Democrats who changed their votes—Moses F. Odell, of New York—went into a Federal job as navy agent in New York City after leaving Congress at the end of the session in 1865. Representative George W. Julian, Republican from Indiana, may have had patronage deals in mind when he wrote, enigmatically, that the success of the measure "depended upon certain negotiations the result of which was not fully assured, and the particulars of which never reached the public." In any event, Lincoln declined to go as far as he might have done in "negotiations" with Congressmen. Representative James Ashley, in charge of the amendment in the House, urged upon him a scheme to get the aid of the New Jersey Democrats. A bill was pending which was intended to curb the monopoly of the Camden and Amboy Railroad in New Jersey, and the railroad company apparently controlled the congressmen from that state. Senator Sumner was behind the anti-monopoly bill. If Sumner would postpone it—so Ashley informed Lincoln—the company "would in return make the New Jersey Democrats help about the amendment, either by their votes or absence." But Lincoln felt he could do nothing with Sumner. He told Ashley that the Senator would become "all the more resolute" if he tried to persuade him to give in. . . .

The Amendment Carries

On January 31, 1865, the proposal came to a final vote in the House. Stevens had set the hour at three o'clock, but Ashley allowed the Democrats to go on speaking until half past three. A group of angry Republicans gathered around Ashley's seat, Thaddeus Stevens among them. His eyes blazing, he shook his finger at Ashley and read him a lecture for giving way, while Ashley's face, according to a witness, looked "as red as a fresh cut of beef." Though a few minutes behind schedule, the roll call duly began.

As the clerk came to the names of the Democrats who the previous session had voted *nay,* and one after another several of them—Baldwin, Coffroth, McAllister, English, Ganson—now voted *aye,* the crowded galleries burst out with repeated and growing applause, and many of the Republicans on the floor joined in it. All together, thirteen Democrats this day voted in favor of the amendment, besides the four who also had voted for it previously. The resolution carried with more than the necessary two-thirds majority. When Speaker Schuyler Colfax announced the result, renewed and intensified cheering was heard, and parliamentary order was forgotten. The House quickly adjourned for the day. Outside, cannon boomed.

From Capitol Hill, Representative Arnold with a group of Lincoln's personal friends went at once to the White House to exchange congratulations with the President. "The passage of the resolution filled his heart with joy," Arnold later recalled. "He saw in it the complete consummation of his own work, the emancipation proclamation."

The next day, February 1, 1865, when the resolution was brought to him for his signature, Lincoln signed it, as seemed perfectly natural for him to do. He, along with Speaker Colfax and Vice President Hannibal Hamlin, had forgotten that the President need not sign a resolution of that kind. On second thought the Senate resolved that "such approval was unnecessary," since the Supreme Court had decided in a case arising in 1798 that the President had "nothing to do" with either the proposal or the adoption of constitutional amendments. Only in a technical sense, however, did Lincoln have nothing to do with this one.

The crowd who, on the evening of the day he signed the resolution, marched to the White House to felicitate him, certainly thought that he had had something to do with it. He had done what he could to eradicate slavery by issuing his proclamation, he told the marchers, but the proclamation "did not meet the evil," or so its critics might maintain. "But this amendment is a King's cure for all the evils. It winds the whole thing up." He could not help congratulating everyone in the crowd, himself, the country, and the whole world upon this "great moral victory."

As the news spread, the old abolitionists were among the most enthusiastic of all who rejoiced throughout the North. To them the President long had seemed timid and ineffectual in dealing with slavery. Now, at last, they could give him unstinted and wholehearted praise. "And to whom is the country more immediately indebted for this

vital and saving amendment of the Constitution than, perhaps to any other man?" So William Lloyd Garrison asked
in the course of a speech to a meeting of celebrators in
Boston. "I believe I may confidently answer," he went on,
"—to the humble railsplitter of Illinois—to the Presidential chainbreaker for millions of the oppressed—to Abraham Lincoln!"

APPENDIX OF DOCUMENTS

Document 1: A House Divided

Lincoln's "House Divided" speech was delivered on June 16, 1858 at the close of the Republican State convention during which Lincoln had been named as Republican candidate for U.S. Senator. The speech criticized many of the measures that Congress had recently passed that extended the reach of slavery into the territories. In this excerpt from that famous speech, Lincoln used a biblical metaphor to explain his concern that slavery had rent the nation and that the Union could not continue with its people divided over the issue of slavery. Prophetically, Lincoln expressed his opinion that the Union would be saved but that it would be either all slave or all free.

"A house divided against itself cannot stand."

I believe this government cannot endure, permanently half *slave* and half *free*.

I do not expect the Union to be *dissolved*—I do not expect the house to *fall*—but I *do* expect it will cease to be divided.

It will become *all* one thing, or *all* the other.

Either the *opponents* of slavery, will arrest the further spread of it, and place it where the public mind shall rest in the belief that it is in course of ultimate extinction; or its advocates will push it forward, till it shall become alike lawful in *all* the States, *old* as well as *new*—*North* as well as *South*.

Abraham Lincoln, "'House Divided' Speech at Springfield, Illinois." *Portable Abraham Lincoln*, ed. by Andrew Delbanco. New York: Viking, 1992.

Document 2: Lincoln's First Inaugural Address

When Lincoln delivered his first inaugural address on March 4, 1861, several Southern states had already threatened to secede from the Union. In his speech, Lincoln attempted to assuage Southern fears that a Republican administration would pose a threat to the South. He claimed to have no legal right to interfere with the states' domestic institutions such as slavery, and promised that he would not use force in maintaining government property in Southern states unless forced to by revolution. Indeed, Lincoln made clear that he would view any attempt at secession as a revolution because the Union was perpetual—it could not be legally broken up unless every state agreed to it. Lincoln concluded with the reminder that North and South were friends, not enemies, and should strive for a peaceful resolution of their differences.

Apprehension seems to exist among the people of the Southern States, that by the accession of a Republican Administration, their property, and their peace, and personal security, are to be endangered. There has never been any reasonable cause for such apprehension. Indeed, the most ample evidence to the contrary has all the while existed, and been open to their inspection. It is found in nearly all the published speeches of him who now addresses you. I do but quote from one of those speeches when I declare that "I have no purpose, directly or indirectly, to interfere with the institution of slavery in the States where it exists. I believe I have no lawful right to do so, and I have no inclination to do so." Those who nominated and elected me did so with full knowledge that I had made this, and many similar declarations, and had never recanted them. And more than this, they placed in the platform, for my acceptance, and as a law to themselves, and to me, the clear and emphatic resolution which I now read:

"*Resolved,* That the maintenance inviolate of the rights of the States, and especially the right of each State to order and control its own domestic institutions according to its own judgment exclusively, is essential to that balance of power on which the perfection and endurance of our political fabric depend; and we denounce the lawless invasion by armed force of the soil of any State or Territory, no matter under what pretext, as among the gravest of crimes."

I now reiterate these sentiments: and in doing so, I only press upon the public attention the most conclusive evidence of which the case is susceptible, that the property, peace and security of no section are to be in anywise endangered by the now incoming Administration. . . .

The Union of These States Is Perpetual
A disruption of the Federal Union heretofore only menaced, is now formidably attempted.

I hold, that in contemplation of universal law, and of the Constitution, the Union of these States is perpetual. Perpetuity is implied, if not expressed, in the fundamental law of all national governments. It is safe to assert that no government proper, ever had a provision in its organic law for its own termination. Continue to execute all the express provisions of our national Constitution, and the Union will endure forever—it being impossible to destroy it, except by some action not provided for in the instrument itself.

Again, if the United States be not a government proper, but an association of States in the nature of contract merely, can it, as a contract, be peaceably unmade, by less than all the parties who made it? One party to a contract may violate it—break it, so to speak; but does it not require all to lawfully rescind it?

Descending from these general principles, we find the proposition that, in legal contemplation, the Union is perpetual, confirmed by the history of the Union itself. The Union is much older than the Constitution. It was formed in fact, by the Articles of Association in 1774. It was matured and continued by the Declaration of Independence in 1776. It was further matured and the faith of all the then thirteen States expressly plighted and engaged that it should be perpetual, by the Articles of Confederation in 1778. And finally, in 1787, one of the declared objects for ordaining and establishing the Constitution, was "*to form a more perfect union.*"

But if destruction of the Union, by one, or by a part only, of the States, be lawfully possible, the Union is *less* perfect than before the Constitution, having lost the vital element of perpetuity.

It follows from these views that no State, upon its own mere motion, can lawfully get out of the Union,—that *resolves* and *ordinances* to that effect are legally void; and that acts of violence, within any State or States, against the authority of the United States, are insurrectionary or revolutionary, according to circumstances.

I therefore consider that, in view of the Constitution and the laws, the Union is unbroken; and, to the extent of my ability, I shall take care, as the Constitution itself expressly enjoins upon me, that the laws of the Union be faithfully executed in all the States. Doing this I deem to be only a simple duty on my part; and I shall perform it, so far as practicable, unless my rightful masters, the American people, shall withhold the requisite means, or, in some authoritative manner, direct the contrary. I trust this will not be regarded as a menace, but only as the declared purpose of the Union that it *will* constitutionally defend, and maintain itself.

In doing this there needs to be no bloodshed or violence; and there shall be none, unless it be forced upon the national authority. The power confided to me, will be used to hold, occupy, and possess the property, and places belonging to the government, and to collect the duties and imposts; but beyond what may be necessary for these objects, there will be no invasion—no using of force against, or among the people anywhere. . . .

We Must Not Be Enemies

In *your* hands, my dissatisfied fellow countrymen, and not in *mine,* is the momentous issue of civil war. The government will not assail *you.* You can have no conflict, without being yourselves the aggressors. *You* have no oath registered in Heaven to destroy the government, while *I* shall have the most solemn one to "preserve, protect and defend" it.

I am loth, to close. We are not enemies, but friends. We must not be enemies. Though passion may have strained, it must not break our bonds of affection. The mystic chords of memory, stretching from every battle-field, and patriot grave, to every living heart and hearth-stone, all over this broad land, will yet swell the chorus of the Union, when again touched, as surely they will be, by the better angels of our nature.

Abraham Lincoln, "First Inaugural Address." *Portable Abraham Lincoln*, ed. by Andrew Delbanco. New York: Viking, 1992.

Document 3: Lincoln's Message to Congress on Compensated Emancipation

In his message to Congress on March 6, 1862, Lincoln unfolded his plan for gradual, compensated emancipation. Lincoln argued that if the loyal border states would accept pecuniary aid in exchange for freeing their slaves, the rebel South would lose hope that the border states would join the Confederacy and the costly war would end. In addition, Lincoln stressed that the program was voluntary and would in no way usurp the rights of the States to manage their own domestic institutions. Lincoln's offer was not accepted by any state, however.

Fellow-citizens of the Senate, and House of Representatives,

I recommend the adoption of a Joint Resolution by your honorable bodies which shall be substantially as follows:

"Resolved that the United States ought to co-operate with any state which may adopt gradual abolishment of slavery, giving to such state pecuniary aid, to be used by such state in it's discretion, to compensate for the inconveniences public and private, produced by such change of system."

If the proposition contained in the resolution does not meet the ap-proval of Congress and the country, there is the end; but if it does command such approval, I deem it of importance that the states and people immediately interested, should be at once distinctly notified of the fact, so that they may begin to consider whether to accept or reject it. The federal government would find it's highest interest in such a measure, as one of the most efficient means of self-preservation. The leaders of the existing insurrection entertain the hope that this government will ultimately be forced to acknowledge the independence of some part of the disaffected region, and that all the slave states North of such part will then say "the Union, for which we have struggled, being already gone, we now choose to go with the Southern section." To deprive them of this hope, substantially ends the rebellion; and the initiation of emancipation completely deprives them of it, as to all the states initiating it. The point is not that *all* the states tolerating slavery would very soon, if at all, initiate emancipation; but that, while the offer is equally made to all, the more Northern shall, by such initiation, make it certain to the more Southern, that in no event, will the former ever join the latter, in their proposed confederacy. I say "initiation" because, in my judgment, gradual, and not sudden emancipation, is better for all. In the mere financial, or pecuniary view, any member of Congress, with the census-tables and Treasury-reports before him, can readily see for himself how very soon the current expenditures of this war would purchase, at fair valuation, all the slaves in any named State. Such a proposition, on the part of the general government, sets up no claim of a right, by federal authority, to interfere with slavery within state limits, referring, as it does, the absolute control of the subject, in each case, to the state and it's people, immediately interested. It is proposed as a matter of perfectly free choice with them.

In the annual message last December, I thought fit to say "The Union must be preserved; and hence all indispensable means must be employed." I said this, not hastily, but deliberately. War has been made, and continues to be, an indispensable means to this end. A practical reacknowledgement of the national authority would render the war unnecessary and it would at once cease. If, however, resistance continues; the war must also continue; and it is impossible to foresee all the incidents, which may attend and all the ruin which may follow it. Such as may seem indispensable, or may obviously promise great efficiency towards ending the struggle, must and will come.

The proposition now made, though an offer only, I hope it may be esteemed no offence to ask whether the pecuniary consideration tendered would not be of more value to the States and private persons concerned, than are the institution, and property in it, in the present aspect of affairs.

While it is true that the adoption of the proposed resolution would be merely initiatory, and not within itself a practical measure, it is recommended in the hope that it would soon lead to important practical results. In full view of my great responsibility to my God, and to my country, I earnestly beg the attention of Congress and the people to the subject.

Abraham Lincoln, "Message to Congress." *Portable Abraham Lincoln*, ed. by Andrew Delbanco. New York: Viking, 1992.

Document 4: Lincoln's Address on Colonization

Speaking to a delegation of African-Americans on August 14, 1862, Lincoln explained his plan to colonize freedmen in Central America. He argued that African-Americans would never be granted equality with Whites in the United States, nor would Whites ever be free from the evil effects of slavery until all African-Americans were gone. Lincoln told the delegation that Central America was a better location to colonize than Liberia because it was closer to the freedman's native U.S. home and had enough natural resources such as coal to provide for their self-reliance.

Perhaps you have long been free, or all your lives. Your race are suffering, in my judgment, the greatest wrong inflicted on any people. But even when you cease to be slaves, you are yet far removed from being placed on an equality with the white race. You are cut off from many of the advantages which the other race enjoy. The aspiration of men is to enjoy equality with the best when free, but on this broad continent, not a single man of your race is made the equal of a single man of ours. Go where you are treated the best, and the ban [slavery] is still upon you.

I do not propose to discuss this, but to present it as a fact with which we have to deal. I cannot alter it if I would. It is a fact, about which we all think and feel alike. I and you. We look to our condition, owing to the existence of the two races on this continent. I need not recount to you the effects upon white men, growing out of the institution of Slavery. I believe in its general evil effects on the white race. See our present condition—the country engaged in war!—our white men cutting one another's throats, none knowing how far it will extend; and then consider what we know to be the truth. But for your race among us there could not be war, although many men engaged on either side do not care for you one way or the other. Nevertheless, I repeat, without the institution of Slavery and the colored race as a basis, the war could not have an existence.

It is better for us both, therefore, to be separated. . . .

The place I am thinking about having for a colony is in Central America. It is nearer to us than Liberia—not much more than one-fourth as far as Liberia, and within seven days' run by steamers. Unlike Liberia it is on a great line of travel—it is a highway. The country is a very excellent one for any people, and with great natural resources and advantages, and especially because of the similarity of climate with your native land—thus being suited to your physical condition. . . .

The practical thing I want to ascertain is, whether I can get a number of able-bodied men, with their wives and children, who are willing to go, when I present evidence of encouragement and protection. Could I get a hundred tolerably intelligent men, with their wives and children, to "cut their own fodder," so to speak? Can I have fifty? If I could find twenty-five able-bodied men, with a mixture of women and children, good things in the family relation, I think I could make a successful commencement.

I want you to let me know whether this can be done or not. This is the practical part of my wish to see you. These are subjects of very great importance, worthy of a month's study, instead of a speech delivered in an hour. I ask you then to consider seriously not pertaining to yourselves merely, nor for your race, and ours, for the present time, but as one of the things, if successfully managed, for the good of mankind.

Abraham Lincoln, "Address on Colonization to a Committee of Colored Men, Washington, D.C."
Portable Abraham Lincoln, ed. by Andrew Delbanco. New York: Viking, 1992.

Document 5: To Horace Greeley: Official Duty Versus Personal Desire

On August 20, 1862, New York Tribune *editor Horace Greeley wrote an open letter to Lincoln called "The Prayer of Twenty Millions." Greeley, presuming to speak for the masses, criticized Lincoln for his conservative policy on slavery and demanded that Lincoln execute the Confiscation Act, which gave freedom to the slaves of rebels. Lincoln responded to Greeley's criticisms by publishing a letter to him in the* National Intelligencer *on August 23, 1862. In the letter, Lincoln stated that his policy had always been to save the Union, and he made clear that he would handle the slavery issue in whatever way necessary to further that end. He claimed that his official duty limited him to saving the Union, regardless of his personal wish that all slaves be free.*

I have just read your open letter of the 19th. addressed to myself through the New York *Tribune*. If there be in it any statements, or assumptions of fact, which I may know to be erroneous, I do not, now and here, controvert them. If there be in it any inferences which I may believe to be falsely drawn, I do not now and here, argue against them. If there be perceptable in it an impatient and dictatorial tone, I waive it in deference to an old friend, whose heart I have always supposed to be right.

As to the policy I "seem to be pursuing" as you say, I have not meant to leave any one in doubt.

I would save the Union. I would save it the shortest way under the Constitution. The sooner the national authority can be restored; the nearer the Union will be "the Union as it was." If there be those who would not save the Union, unless they could at the same time *save* slavery, I do not agree with them. If there be those who would not save the Union unless they could at the same time *destroy* slavery, I do not agree with them. My paramount object in this struggle *is* to save the Union, and is *not* either to save or to destroy slavery. If I could save the Union without freeing *any* slave I would do it, and if I could save it by freeing *all* the slaves I would do it; and if I could save it by freeing some and leaving others alone I would also do that. What I do about slavery, and the colored race, I do because I believe it helps to save the Union; and what I forbear, I forbear because I do *not* believe it would help to save the Union. I shall do *less* whenever I shall believe what I am doing hurts the cause, and I shall do *more* whenever I shall believe doing more will help the cause. I shall try to correct errors when shown to be errors; and I shall adopt new views so fast as they shall appear to be true views.

I have here stated my purpose according to my view of *official* duty; and I intend no modification of my oft-expressed *personal* wish that all men every where could be free.

Abraham Lincoln, "To Horace Greeley." *Portable Abraham Lincoln*, ed. by Andrew Delbanco. New York: Viking, 1992.

Document 6: Proclamation Suspending the Writ of Habeas Corpus

Lincoln officially suspended the writ of habeas corpus on September 24, 1862, in order to help the Union war effort. The writ of habeas corpus allows anyone arrested to ask for a hearing in order to determine the justness of the arrest. However, during the Civil War, Southern sympathizers who were arrested and put in military prisons would most likely be released if the writ remained in effect because the courts had become too busy to handle the numerous cases they had. Lincoln worried that such prisoners, once released, would resume their anti-war activities.

Whereas, it has become necessary to call into service not only volunteers but also portions of the militia of the States by draft in order to suppress the insurrection existing in the United States, and disloyal persons are not adequately restrained by the ordinary processes of law from hindering this measure and from giving aid and comfort in various ways to the insurrection;

Now, therefore, be it ordered, first, that during the existing insurrection and as a necessary measure for suppressing the same, all Rebels and Insurgents, their aiders and abettors within the United States, and all persons discouraging volunteer enlistments, resisting militia drafts, or guilty of any disloyal practice, affording aid and comfort to Rebels against the authority of the United States, shall be subject to martial law and liable to trial and punishment by Courts Martial or Military Commission:

Second. That the Writ of Habeas Corpus is suspended in respect to all persons arrested, or who are now, or hereafter during the rebellion shall be, imprisoned in any fort, camp, arsenal, military prison, or other place of confinement by any military authority or by the sentence of any Court Martial or Military Commission.

In witness whereof, I have hereunto set my hand, and caused the seal of the United States to be affixed.

Done at the City of Washington this twenty fourth day of September, in the year of our Lord one thousand eight hundred and sixty-two.

Abraham Lincoln, "Proclamation Suspending the Writ of Habeas Corpus." *Portable Abraham Lincoln*, ed. by Andrew Delbanco. New York: Viking, 1992.

Document 7: The Final Emancipation Proclamation

On September 22, 1862, Lincoln issued the Preliminary Emancipation Proclamation wherein he pronounced his intent to free all slaves within states still in rebellion on January 1, 1863. As promised, the president issued the Final Emancipation Proclamation in January and specified in which rebel states the slaves would be freed. Lincoln encouraged the freed slaves to join in the Union's war effort, which Lincoln believed would demoralize the South and help the North win the war. According to Lincoln, his position as commander-in-chief gave him the authority to take such a step in order to help suppress the rebellion. The legalese with which the document is written indicates Lincoln's desire to have the proclamation viewed as a war document only, not a general pronouncement of total emancipation, which he was as yet unprepared to make.

Whereas, on the twentysecond day of September, in the year of our Lord one thousand eight hundred and sixty two, a proclamation was issued by the President of the United States, containing, among other things, the following, to wit:

> "That on the first day of January, in the year of our Lord one thousand eight hundred and sixty-three, all persons held as slaves within any State or designated part of a State, the people whereof shall then be in rebellion against the United States, shall be then, thenceforward, and forever free; and the Executive Government of the United States, including the military and naval authority thereof,

will recognize and maintain the freedom of such persons, and will do no act or acts to repress such persons, or any of them, in any efforts they may make for their actual freedom.

"That the Executive will, on the first day of January aforesaid, by proclamation, designate the States and parts of States, if any, in which the people thereof, respectively, shall then be in rebellion against the United States; and the fact that any State, or the people thereof, shall on that day be, in good faith, represented in the Congress of the United States by members chosen thereto at elections wherein a majority of the qualified voters of such State shall have participated, shall, in the absence of strong countervailing testimony, be deemed conclusive evidence that such State, and the people thereof, are not then in rebellion against the United States."

Now, therefore I, Abraham Lincoln, President of the United States, by virtue of the power in me vested as Commander-in-Chief, of the Army and Navy of the United States in time of actual armed rebellion against authority and government of the United States, and as a fit and necessary war measure for suppressing said rebellion, do, on this first day of January, in the year of our Lord one thousand eight hundred and sixty three, and in accordance with my purpose so to do publicly proclaimed for the full period of one hundred days, from the day first above mentioned, order and designate as the States and parts of States wherein the people thereof respectively, are this day in rebellion against the United States, the following, to wit:

Arkansas, Texas, Louisiana, (except the Parishes of St. Bernard, Plaquemines, Jefferson, St. Johns, St. Charles, St. James, Ascension, Assumption, Terrebonne, Lafourche, St. Mary, St. Martin, and Orleans, including the City of New-Orleans) Mississippi, Alabama, Florida, Georgia, South-Carolina, North-Carolina, and Virginia, (except the fortyeight counties designated as West Virginia, and also the counties of Berkley, Accomac, Northampton, Elizabeth-City, York, Princess Ann, and Norfolk, including the cities of Norfolk & Portsmouth); and which excepted parts are, for the present, left precisely as if this proclamation were not issued.

And by virtue of the power, and for the purpose aforesaid, I do order and declare that all persons held as slaves within said designated States, and parts of States, are, and henceforward shall be free; and that the Executive government of the United States, including the military and naval authorities thereof, will recognize and maintain the freedom of said persons.

And I hereby enjoin upon the people so declared to be free to abstain from all violence, unless in necessary self-defence; and I recommend to them that, in all cases when allowed, they labor faithfully for reasonable wages.

And I further declare and make known, that such persons of suitable condition, will be received into the armed service of the United States to garrison forts, positions, stations, and other places, and to man vessels of all sorts in said service.

And upon this act, sincerely believed to be an act of justice, warranted by the Constitution, upon military necessity, I invoke the considerate judgment of mankind, and the gracious favor of Almighty God.

In witness whereof, I have hereunto set my hand and caused the seal of the United States to be affixed.

Done at the City of Washington, this first day of January, in the year of our Lord one thousand eight hundred and sixty three.

Abraham Lincoln, "Final Emancipation Proclamation." *Portable Abraham Lincoln*, ed. by Andrew Delbanco. New York: Viking, 1992.

Document 8: The Gettysburg Address

Lincoln gave the Gettysburg address at the dedication of the Cemetery at Gettysburg on November 19, 1863. In this speech he gave tribute to the Union soldiers who had died at the battle of Gettysburg, and he asked the American people to renew their devotion to the preservation of the world's first experiment in democracy.

Four score and seven years ago our fathers brought forth on this continent, a new nation, conceived in Liberty, and dedicated to the proposition that all men are created equal.

Now we are engaged in a great civil war, testing whether, that nation, or any nation so conceived and so dedicated, can long endure. We are met on a great battle-field of that war. We have come to dedicate a portion of that field, as a final resting place for those who here gave their lives that that nation might live. It is altogether fitting and proper that we should do this.

But, in a larger sense, we can not dedicate—we can not consecrate—we can not hallow—this ground. The brave men, living and dead, who struggled here, have consecrated it, far above our poor power to add or detract. The world will little note, nor long remember what we say here, but it can never forget what they did here. It is for us the living, rather, to be dedicated here to the unfinished work which they who fought here have thus far so nobly advanced. It is rather for us to be here dedicated to the great task remaining before us—that from these honored dead we take increased devotion to that cause for which they gave the last full measure of devotion—that we here highly resolve that these dead shall not have died in vain—that this nation, under God, shall have a new birth of freedom—and that government of the people, by the people, for the people, shall not perish from the earth.

Abraham Lincoln, "Address at Gettysburg, Pennsylvania." *Portable Abraham Lincoln*, ed. by Andrew Delbanco. New York: Viking, 1992.

Document 9: The "10 Percent Plan"

The Proclamation of Amnesty and Reconstruction, which Lincoln issued on December 8, 1863, outlines his "10 Percent Plan" for reintroducing the seceded states back into the Union. Lincoln proclaimed a general pardon for citizens living in rebel states except those who directly aided the rebellion, such as Confederate officers or Southern senators who left Congress when secession began. Lincoln announced that any state that obtained an oath of loyalty from 10 percent of its voters would be readmitted into the Union. He encouraged—but did not mandate—that readmitted states provide security and education to the freed slaves.

I, Abraham Lincoln, President of the United States, do proclaim, declare, and make known to all persons who have, directly or by implication, participated in the existing rebellion, except as hereinafter excepted, that a full pardon is hereby granted to them and each of them, with restoration of all rights of property, except as to slaves, and in property cases where rights of third parties shall have intervened, and upon the condition that every such person shall take and subscribe an oath, and thenceforward keep and maintain said oath inviolate; and which oath shall be registered for permanent preservation, and shall be of the tenor and effect following, to wit:

"I,——, do solemnly swear, in presence of Almighty God, that I will henceforth faithfully support, protect and defend the Constitution of the United States, and the union of the States thereunder; and that I will, in like manner, abide by and faithfully support all acts of Congress passed during the existing rebellion with reference to slaves, so long and so far as not repealed, modified or held void by Congress, or by decision of the Supreme Court; and that I will, in like manner, abide by and faithfully support all proclamations of the President made during the existing rebellion having reference to slaves, so long and so far as not modified or declared void by decision of the Supreme Court. So help me God."

The persons excepted from the benefits of the foregoing provisions are all who are, or shall have been, civil or diplomatic officers or agents of the so-called confederate government; all who have left judicial stations under the United States to aid the rebellion; all who are, or shall have been, military or naval officers of said so-called confederate government above the rank of colonel in the army, or of lieutenant in the navy; all who left seats in the United States Congress to aid the rebellion; all who resigned commissions in the army or navy of the United States, and afterwards aided the rebellion; and all who have engaged in any way in treating colored persons or white persons, in charge of such, otherwise than lawfully as prisoners of war, and which persons may have been found in the United States service, as soldiers, seamen, or in any other capacity.

And I do further proclaim, declare, and make known, that whenever, in any of the States of Arkansas, Texas, Louisiana, Mississippi, Tennessee, Alabama, Georgia, Florida, South Carolina, and North Carolina, a number of persons, not less than one-tenth in number of the votes cast in such State at the Presidential election of the year of our Lord one thousand eight hundred and sixty, each having taken the oath aforesaid and not having since violated it, and being a qualified voter by the election law of the State existing immediately before the so-called act of secession, and excluding all others, shall re-establish a State government which shall be republican, and in no wise contravening said oath, such shall be recognized as the true government of the State, and the State shall receive thereunder the benefits of the constitutional provision which declares that "The United States shall guaranty to every State in this union a republican form of government, and shall protect each of them against invasion; and, on application of the legislature, or the executive, (when the legislature cannot be convened,) against domestic violence."

And I do further proclaim, declare, and make known that any provision which may be adopted by such State government in relation to the freed people of such State, which shall recognize and declare their permanent freedom, provide for their education, and which may yet be consistent, as a temporary arrangement, with their present condition as a laboring, landless, and homeless class, will not be objected to by the national Executive. And it is suggested as not improper, that, in constructing a loyal State government in any State, the name of the State, the boundary, the subdivisions, the constitution, and the general code of laws, as before the rebellion, be maintained, subject only to the modifications made necessary by the conditions hereinbefore stated, and such others, if any, not contravening said conditions, and which may be deemed expedient by those framing the new State government. . . .

Given under my hand at the city of Washington, the 8th. day of December, A.D. one thousand eight hundred and sixty-three.

Abraham Lincoln, "Proclamation of Amnesty and Reconstruction." *Portable Abraham Lincoln*, ed. by Andrew Delbanco. New York: Viking, 1992.

Document 10: Letter to Albert G. Hodges on Arming Freed Slaves

On April 4, 1864, Lincoln wrote a letter to Albert G. Hodges that reiterated the views he had expressed orally during a previous meeting with him. In the letter, Lincoln stated that his highest duty as president was to preserve the Union by whatever means possible. He explained that national emergencies often made executive actions that would previously have been unconstitutional completely justified. Specifically, Lincoln justifies his executive order that freed slaves be armed in order to fight for the Union cause.

"I am naturally anti-slavery. If slavery is not wrong, nothing is wrong. I can not remember when I did not so think, and feel. And yet I have never understood that the Presidency conferred upon me an unrestricted right to act officially upon this judgment and feeling. It was in the oath I took that I would, to the best of my ability, preserve, protect, and defend the Constitution of the United States. I could not take the office without taking the oath. Nor was it my view that I might take an oath to get power, and break the oath in using the power. I understood, too, that in ordinary civil administration this oath even forbade me to practically indulge my primary abstract judgment on the moral question of slavery. I had publicly declared this many times, and in many ways. And I aver that, to this day, I have done no official act in mere deference to my abstract judgment and feeling on slavery. I did understand however, that my oath to preserve the constitution to the best of my ability, imposed upon me the duty of preserving, by every indispensable means, that government—that nation—of which that constitution was the organic law. Was it possible to lose the nation, and yet preserve the constitution? By general law life *and* limb must be protected; yet often a limb must be amputated to save a life; but a life is never wisely given to save a limb. I felt that measures, otherwise unconstitutional, might become lawful, by becoming indispensable to the preservation of the constitution, through the preservation of the nation. Right or wrong, I assumed this ground, and now avow it. I could not feel that, to the best of my ability, I had even tried to preserve the constitution, if, to save slavery, or any minor matter, I should permit the wreck of government, country, and Constitution all together. When, early in the war, General John C. Fremont attempted military emancipation, I forbade it, because I did not then think it an indispensable necessity. When a little later, General Cameron, then Secretary of War, suggested the arming of the blacks, I objected, because I did not yet think it an indispensable necessity. When, still later, General David Hunter attempted military emancipation, I again forbade it, because I did not yet think the indispensable necessity had come. When, in March, and May, and July 1862 I made earnest, and successive appeals to the border states to favor compensated emancipation, I believed the indispensable necessity for military emancipation, and arming the blacks would come, unless averted by that measure. They declined the proposition; and I was, in my best judgment, driven to the alternative of either surrendering the Union, and with it, the Constitution, or of laying strong hand upon the colored element. I chose the latter. In choosing it, I hoped for greater gain than loss; but of this, I was not entirely confident. More than a year of trial now shows no loss by it in our foreign relations, none in our home popular sentiment, none in our white military force,—no loss by it any how or any where. On the contrary, it shows a gain of quite a hundred and thirty thousand soldiers, seamen, and laborers. These are palpable facts, about which, as facts, there can be no cavilling. We have the men; and we could not have had them without the measure.

"And now let any Union man who complains of the measure, test himself by writing down in one line that he is for subduing the rebellion by force of arms; and in the next, that he is for taking these hundred and thirty thousand men from the Union side, and placing them where they would be but for the measure he condemns. If he can not face his case so stated, it is only because he can not face the truth."

In telling this tale I attempt no compliment to my own sagacity. I claim not to have controlled events, but confess plainly that events have controlled me. Now, at the end of three years struggle the nation's condition is not what either party, or any man devised, or expected. God alone can claim it. Whither it is tending seems plain. If God now wills the removal of a great wrong, and wills also that we of the North as well as you of the South, shall pay fairly for our complicity in that wrong, impartial history will find therein new cause to attest and revere the justice and goodness of God.

Abraham Lincoln, "To Albert G. Hodges." *Portable Abraham Lincoln*, ed. by Andrew Delbanco. New York: Viking, 1992.

Document 11: The Importance of Free Elections

At a serenade honoring Lincoln on November 10, 1864, the newly re-elected president responded with praise for the country. The fact that a democracy was able to hold free elections in the middle of a civil war showed the nation's strength and viability, he maintained. Many critics within the Republican party had worked to prevent Lincoln from getting the Republican nomination for president. He acknowledged the unfortunate political strife that occurred during the election but claimed that it was no inherent fault of the Union.

It has long been a grave question whether any government, not *too* strong for the liberties of its people, can be strong *enough* to maintain its own existence, in great emergencies.

On this point the present rebellion brought our republic to a severe test; and a presidential election occurring in regular course during the rebellion added not a little to the strain. If the loyal people, *united*, were put to the utmost of their strength by the rebellion, must they not fail when *divided*, and partially paralized, by a political war among themselves?

But the election was a necessity.

We can not have free government without elections; and if the rebellion could force us to forego, or postpone a national election, it might fairly claim to have already conquered and ruined us. The strife of the election is but human-nature practically applied to the facts of the case. What has occurred in this case, must ever recur in similar cases. Human-nature will not change. In any future great national trial, compared with the men of this, we shall have as weak, and as strong; as silly and as wise; as bad and good. Let us, therefore, study the incidents of this, as philosophy to learn wisdom from, and none of them as wrongs to be revenged.

But the election, along with its incidental, and undesirable strife, has done good too. It has demonstrated that a people's government can sustain a national election, in the midst of a great civil war. Until now it has not been known to the world that this was a possibility. It shows also how *sound*, and how *strong* we still are. It shows that, even among candidates of the same party, he who is most devoted to the Union, and most opposed to treason, can receive most of the people's votes. It shows also, to the extent yet known, that we have more men now, than we had when the war began. Gold is good in its place; but living, brave, patriotic men, are better than gold.

But the rebellion continues; and now that the election is over, may not all, having a common interest, re-unite in a common effort, to save our common country? For my own part I have striven, and shall strive to avoid placing any obstacle in the way. So long as I have been here I have not willingly planted a thorn in any man's bosom.

While I am deeply sensible to the high compliment of a re-election; and duly grateful, as I trust, to Almighty God for having directed my countrymen to a right conclusion, as I think, for their own good, it adds nothing to my satisfaction that any other man may be disappointed or pained by the result.

May I ask those who have not differed with me, to join with me, in this same spirit towards those who have?

And now, let me close by asking three hearty cheers for our brave soldiers and seamen and their gallant and skilful commanders.

Abraham Lincoln, "Response to Serenade, Washington, D.C." *Portable Abraham Lincoln*, ed. by Andrew Delbanco. New York: Viking, 1992.

Document 12: Lincoln's Second Inaugural Address

In Lincoln's second inaugural address, given on March 4, 1865, the president made clear that slavery was the cause of the war. He claimed that the South started the war in order to protect slavery, while the North accepted the war in order to limit slavery's expansion. Furthermore, the president argued that the war was God's punishment on the American people for tolerating slavery. In spite of the blame he placed on the South for starting the war, however, Lincoln urged reconciliation without vengeance.

Fellow Countrymen:

At this second appearing to take the oath of the presidential office, there is less occasion for an extended address than there was at the first. Then a statement, somewhat in detail, of a course to be pursued, seemed fitting and proper. Now, at the expiration of four years, during which public declarations have been constantly called forth on every point and phase of the great contest which still absorbs the attention, and engrosses the energies of the nation, little that is new could be presented. The progress of our arms, upon which all else chiefly depends, is as well known to the public as to myself; and it is, I trust, reasonably satisfactory and encouraging to all. With high hope for the future, no prediction in regard to it is ventured.

On the occasion corresponding to this four years ago, all thoughts were anxiously directed to an impending civil-war. All dreaded it—all sought to avert it. While the inaugeral address was being delivered from this place, devoted altogether to *saving* the Union without war, insurgent agents were in the city seeking to *destroy* it without war—

seeking to dissolve the Union, and divide effects, by negotiation. Both parties deprecated war; but one of them would *make* war rather than let the nation survive; and the other would *accept* war rather than let it perish. And the war came.

One eighth of the whole population were colored slaves, not distributed generally over the Union, but localized in the Southern part of it. These slaves constituted a peculiar and powerful interest. All knew that this interest was, somehow, the cause of the war. To strengthen, perpetuate, and extend this interest was the object for which the insurgents would rend the Union, even by war; while the government claimed no right to do more than to restrict the territorial enlargement of it. Neither party expected for the war, the magnitude, or the duration, which it has already attained. Neither anticipated that the *cause* of the conflict might cease with, or even before, the conflict itself should cease. Each looked for an easier triumph, and a result less fundamental and astounding. Both read the same Bible, and pray to the same God; and each invokes His aid against the other. It may seem strange that any men should dare to ask a just God's assistance in wringing their bread from the sweat of other men's faces; but let us judge not that we be not judged. The prayers of both could not be answered; that of neither has been answered fully. The Almighty has His own purposes. "Woe unto the world because of offences! for it must needs be that offences come; but woe to that man by whom the offence cometh!" If we shall suppose that American Slavery is one of those offences which, in the providence of God, must needs come, but which, having continued through His appointed time, He now wills to remove, and that He gives to both North and South, this terrible war, as the woe due to those by whom the offence came, shall we discern therein any departure from those divine attributes which the believers in a Living God always ascribe to Him? Fondly do we hope—fervently do we pray—that this mighty scourge of war may speedily pass away. Yet, if God wills that it continue, until all the wealth piled by the bond-man's two hundred and fifty years of unrequited toil shall be sunk, and until every drop of blood drawn with the lash, shall be paid by another drawn with the sword, as was said three thousand years ago, so still it must be said "the judgments of the Lord, are true and righteous altogether."

With malice toward none; with charity for all; with firmness in the right, as God gives us to see the right, let us strive on to finish the work we are in; to bind up the nation's wounds; to care for him who shall have borne the battle, and for his widow, and his orphan—to do all

which may achieve and cherish a just, and a lasting peace, among ourselves, and with all nations.

Abraham Lincoln, "Second Inaugural Address." *Portable Abraham Lincoln*, ed. by Andrew Delbanco.
New York: Viking, 1992.

Document 13: Lincoln's Speech on Reconstruction

*In the following excerpt from Lincoln's last public address, which he de-
livered in Washington, D.C., on April 11, 1865, the president defends his
reconstruction plan in Louisiana. Lincoln admitted that the Louisiana
experiment wasn't perfect—the state got relatively few people to sign the
oath of loyalty, for example—but he argued that the progress that had
been made there should not be undone.*

By [the recent military successes at Petersburg and Richmond] the re-
inauguration of the national authority—reconstruction—which has
had a large share of thought from the first, is pressed much more
closely upon our attention. It is fraught with great difficulty. Unlike the
case of a war between independent nations, there is no authorized
organ for us to treat with. No one man has authority to give up the rebellion for any other man. We simply must begin with, and mould
from, disorganized and discordant elements. Nor is it a small additional embarrassment that we, the loyal people, differ among ourselves
as to the mode, manner, and means of reconstruction. . . .

The amount of constituency, so to speak, on which the new
Louisiana government rests, would be more satisfactory to all, if it
contained fifty, thirty, or even twenty thousand, instead of only about
twelve thousand, as it does. It is also unsatisfactory to some that the
elective franchise is not given to the colored man. I would myself prefer that it were now conferred on the very intelligent, and on those
who serve our cause as soldiers. Still the question is not whether the
Louisiana government, as it stands, is quite all that is desirable. The
question is "Will it be wiser to take it as it is, and help to improve it; or
to reject, and disperse it?" "Can Louisiana be brought into proper
practical relation with the Union *sooner* by *sustaining*, or by *discarding*
her new State Government?"

Some twelve thousand voters in the heretofore slave-state of
Louisiana have sworn allegiance to the Union, assumed to be the rightful political power of the State, held elections, organized a State government, adopted a free-state constitution, giving the benefit of public schools equally to black and white, and empowering the Legislature
to confer the elective franchise upon the colored man. Their Legisla-

ture has already voted to ratify the constitutional amendment recently passed by Congress, abolishing slavery throughout the nation. These
twelve thousand persons are thus fully committed to the Union, and to
perpetual freedom in the state—committed to the very things, and
nearly all the things the nation wants—and they ask the nation's
recognition, and it's assistance to make good their committal. Now, if
we reject, and spurn them, we do our utmost to disorganize and disperse them. We in effect say to the white men "You are worthless, or
worse—we will neither help you, nor be helped by you." To the blacks
we say "This cup of liberty which these, your old masters, hold to your
lips, we will dash from you, and leave you to the chances of gathering
the spilled and scattered contents in some vague and undefined when,
where, and how." If this course, discouraging and paralyzing both
white and black, has any tendency to bring Louisiana into proper practical relations with the Union, I have, so far, been unable to perceive it.
If, on the contrary, we recognize, and sustain the new government of
Louisiana the converse of all this is made true. We encourage the
hearts, and nerve the arms of the twelve thousand to adhere to their
work, and argue for it, and proselyte for it, and fight for it, and feed it,
and grow it, and ripen it to a complete success. The colored man too,
in seeing all united for him, is inspired with vigilance, and energy, and
daring, to the same end. Grant that he desires the elective franchise,
will he not attain it sooner by saving the already advanced steps toward
it, than by running backward over them? Concede that the new government of Louisiana is only to what it should be as the egg is to the
fowl, we shall sooner have the fowl by hatching the egg than by smash-
ing it? Again, if we reject Louisiana, we also reject one vote in favor of
the proposed [thirteenth] amendment [abolishing slavery] to the national constitution. To meet this proposition, it has been argued that
no more than three fourths of those States which have not attempted
secession are necessary to validly ratify the amendment. I do not com-
mit myself against this, further than to say that such a ratification
would be questionable, and sure to be persistently questioned; while a
ratification by three fourths of all the States would be unquestioned
and unquestionable.

I repeat the question. "Can Louisiana be brought into proper practical relation with the Union *sooner* by *sustaining* or by *discarding* her
new State Government"?

What has been said of Louisiana will apply generally to other States.
And yet so great peculiarities pertain to each state; and such important
and sudden changes occur in the same state; and, withal, so new and

unprecedented is the whole case, that no exclusive, and inflexible plan can safely be prescribed as to details and collaterals. Such exclusive, and inflexible plan, would surely become a new entanglement. Important principles may, and must, be inflexible.

In the present *"situation"* as the phrase goes, it may be my duty to make some new announcement to the people of the South. I am considering, and shall not fail to act, when satisfied that action will be proper.

Abraham Lincoln, "Speech on Reconstruction, Washington, D.C." *Portable Abraham Lincoln*, ed. by Andrew Delbanco. New York: Viking, 1992.

CHRONOLOGY

FEBRUARY 12, 1809
Lincoln is born in a log cabin on a farm in Hardin County, Kentucky.

1830
The Lincoln family moves to Illinois in search of more fertile farm land.

1832
Lincoln declares himself candidate for the Illinois House of Representatives but loses.

1833
Lincoln is named postmaster.

1834
Lincoln wins in his second run for the Illinois House of Representatives.

1837
Lincoln is admitted to the Bar.

1842
Lincoln marries Mary Todd of Lexington, Kentucky.

1843
Lincoln runs unsuccessfully for Congress.

1846
Lincoln is elected to his only term as a U.S. Congressional representative.

1848
Lincoln, tired of politics, returns home to Illinois to practice law.

1854
Passage of the Kansas-Nebraska Act incites Lincoln to return to politics; Lincoln is re-elected to the Illinois House of Representatives but refuses the post in order to run for the U.S. Senate.

1856
Lincoln joins and helps found the Republican party.

1857
Lincoln denounces the Dred Scott Decision, which decreed that slaves are not citizens and that Congress cannot forbid slavery in the territories.

1858
Lincoln engages in a series of debates with Democrat Stephen Douglas during their campaigns for the U.S. Senate.

JUNE 16, 1858
Lincoln gives his "House Divided" speech at the Republican state convention.

NOVEMBER 1860
Lincoln is elected as the sixteenth president of the United States.

DECEMBER 1860
South Carolina, Mississippi, Florida, Alabama, Georgia, Louisiana, and Texas secede.

MARCH 4, 1861
Lincoln is inaugurated as president.

MARCH 29, 1861
Lincoln orders preparation of the Fort Sumter relief expedition.

APRIL 12–13, 1861
Fort Sumter is bombarded and eventually surrenders; Civil War begins.

APRIL 1861
Tennessee, Arkansas, North Carolina, and Virginia secede.

APRIL 15, 1861
Lincoln declares a state of insurrection and calls for 75,000 militia.

APRIL 19, 1861
Lincoln proclaims a blockade of the Southern coast.

AUGUST 6, 1861
Lincoln signs the First Confiscation Act, which frees the slaves of rebels.

AUGUST 30, 1861
Lincoln revokes General John C. Frémont's proclamation declaring martial law and freeing slaves in Missouri.

MARCH 6, 1862
Lincoln proposes gradual emancipation to Congress.

MAY 9, 1862
Lincoln revokes General David Hunter's proclamation freeing slaves in South Carolina, Georgia, and Florida.

JULY 12, 1862
Lincoln fails to persuade the border states to accept his plan for gradual, compensated emancipation.

JULY 17, 1862
Lincoln signs the Second Confiscation Act, which frees the slaves of rebels.

AUGUST 14, 1862
Lincoln pitches his colonization plan to a delegation of African Americans.

SEPTEMBER 22, 1862
Lincoln issues the preliminary Emancipation Proclamation.

SEPTEMBER 24, 1862
Lincoln issues the Proclamation Suspending the Writ of Habeas Corpus.

JANUARY 1, 1863
Lincoln issues the final Emancipation Proclamation.

MARCH 3, 1863
Congress passes the Conscription Act, which assigns quotas for drafting men into the Union army.

JULY 13–16
In New York, draft riots erupt, protesting draft quotas.

NOVEMBER 19, 1863
Lincoln issues the Gettysburg Address.

DECEMBER 8, 1863
Lincoln issues the Proclamation of Amnesty and Reconstruction, which outlines his 10 Percent Plan.

JUNE 7, 1864
Lincoln receives the Republican nomination for president and chooses Andrew Johnson as his running-mate.

JULY 4, 1864
Lincoln pocket-vetoes the Wade-Davis Reconstruction bill.

AUGUST 5, 1864
The Wade-Davis manifesto is issued, which criticizes Lincoln's Reconstruction plan.

AUGUST 18–30, 1864
The Republican party threatens to drop Lincoln as the presidential candidate due to conflict over Reconstruction.

NOVEMBER 8, 1864
Lincoln is re-elected president.

JANUARY 31, 1865
Congress passes the Thirteenth Amendment abolishing slavery.

MARCH 4, 1865
Lincoln is inaugurated for his second term as president.

APRIL 9, 1865
Confederate general Robert E. Lee surrenders to Union general Ulysses S. Grant at Appomattox, ending the Civil War.

APRIL 11, 1865
Lincoln gives his last public address defending his Reconstruction plan in Louisiana.

APRIL 14, 1865
Lincoln is shot by John Wilkes Booth at Ford's Theater; the president dies the next morning.

DECEMBER 1865
The Thirteenth Amendment is ratified by the states.

1892
Lincoln's birthday is made a national holiday.

MAY 30, 1922
The Lincoln Memorial is dedicated in Washington, D.C.

FOR FURTHER RESEARCH

ERIC ANDERSON AND ALFRED A. MOSS, JR. EDS., *The Facts of Reconstruction: Essays in Honor of John Hope Franklin*. Baton Rouge, LA: Louisiana State University Press, 1991.

ROY P. BASLER, ED., *Abraham Lincoln: His Speeches and Writings*. Cleveland, OH: World Publishing, 1946.

LERONE BENNETT JR., *Forced into Glory: Abraham Lincoln's White Dream*. Chicago: Johnson Publishing, 2000.

GABOR S. BORITT, *Abraham Lincoln, War Opponent and War President*. Gettysburg, PA: Gettysburg College, 1987.

GABOR S. BORITT, ED., *Lincoln, the War President: The Gettysburg Lectures*. New York: Oxford University Press, 1992.

GABOR S. BORITT, ED., *Why the Civil War Came*. New York: Oxford University Press, 1996.

HODDING CARTER, *The Angry Scar: The Story of Reconstruction*. Garden City, NY: Doubleday, 1959.

WILLIAM CATTON AND BRUCE CATTON, *Two Roads to Sumter*. New York: McGraw-Hill, 1963.

RICHARD N. CURRENT, *Lincoln and the First Shot*. Philadelphia, PA: Lippincott, 1963.

ANDREW DELBANCO, ED., *Portable Abraham Lincoln*. New York: Viking, 1992.

WILLIAM ARCHIBALD DUNNING, *Essays on the Civil War and Reconstruction*. New York: Harper and Row, 1965.

DON FEHRENBACHER, *The Leadership of Abraham Lincoln*. New York: Wiley, 1970.

ERIC FONER, *Reconstruction: America's Unfinished Revolution*. New York: Harper and Row, 1988.

JOHN HOPE FRANKLIN, *The Emancipation Proclamation*. Garden City, NY: Doubleday, 1963.

GEORGE M. FREDERICKSON, ED., *A Nation Divided: Problems and Issues of the Civil War and Reconstruction.* Minneapolis, MN: Burgess Publishing, 1975.

NORTON GARFINKLE, *Lincoln and the Coming of Civil War.* Boston: Heath, 1959.

WILLIAM HESSELTINE, *Lincoln's Plan of Reconstruction.* Tuscaloosa, AL: Confederate Publishing Company, 1960.

HARRY V. JAFFA, *A New Birth of Freedom: Lincoln and the Coming of the Civil War.* New York: Rowman and Littlefield, 2000.

HOWARD JONES, *Abraham Lincoln and a New Birth of Freedom: The Union and Slavery in the Diplomacy of the Civil War.* Lincoln, NE: University of Nebraska, 1999.

ROBERT HUHN JONES, *Fields of Conflict: The Civil War and Reconstruction in America.* Malabar, FL: Krieger Publishing, 1998.

MAURY KLEIN, *Days of Defiance: Sumter, Secession, and the Coming of Civil War.* New York: Knopf, 1997.

DAVID E. LONG, *The Jewel of Liberty: Abraham Lincoln's Re-Election and the End of Slavery.* Mechanicsburg, PA: Stackpole Books, 1994.

CHARLES H. MCCARTHY, *Lincoln's Plan of Reconstruction.* New York: AMS Press, 1966.

PEYTON MCCRARY, *Abraham Lincoln and Reconstruction: The Louisiana Experiment.* Princeton, NJ: Princeton University Press, 1978.

JAMES M. MCPHERSON, *Battle Cry of Freedom: The Civil War Era.* New York: Oxford University Press, 1988.

JAMES M. MCPHERSON, *Ordeal by Fire: The Civil War and Reconstruction.* New York: Knopf, 1982.

JAMES MCPHERSON, *"We Cannot Escape History": Lincoln and the Last Best Hope of Earth.* Urbana, IL: University of Illinois Press, 1995.

HERBERT MITGANG, *Abraham Lincoln, A Press Portrait: His Life and Times from the Original Newspaper Documents of the*

Union, the Confederacy, and Europe. Chicago: Quandrangle Books, 1971.

MARK E. NEELEY JR., *The Last Best Hope of Earth: Abraham Lincoln and the Promise of America*. Cambridge, MA: Harvard University Press, 1993.

PHILLIP S. PALUDAN, *The Presidency of Abraham Lincoln*. Lawrence, Kansas: University of Kansas Press, 1994.

DAVID MORRIS POTTER, *Lincoln and His Party in the Secession Crisis*. New Haven: Yale University Press, 1967.

CHARLES W. RAMSDELL, *Behind the Lines in the Southern Confederacy*. Baton Rouge, LA: Louisiana State University, 1944.

J.G. RANDALL AND DAVID HERBERT DONALD, *The Civil War and Reconstruction*. Lexington, MA: Heath, 1969.

J.G. RANDALL, *Constitutional Problems Under Lincoln*. Glouster, MA: Peter Smith, 1963.

J.G. RANDALL, *Lincoln, the President*. New York: Dodd and Meade, 1946.

JAMES A. RAWLEY, *Abraham Lincoln and a Nation Worth Fighting For*. Wheeling, IL: Harlan Davidson, 1996.

DEAN SPRAGUE, *Freedom Under Lincoln*. Boston, MA: Houghton Mifflin, 1965.

JOHN SHIPLEY TILLEY, *Lincoln Takes Command*. Chapel Hill, NC: University of North Carolina Press, 1941.

HANS TREFOUSSE, *Lincoln's Decision for Emancipation*. Philadelphia, PA: Lippincott, 1975.

HANS TREFOUSSE, *The Radical Republicans: Lincoln's Vanguard for Social Justice*. New York: Knopf, 1969.

HANS TREFOUSSE, *Reconstruction: America's First Effort at Racial Democracy*. Huntington, NY: R. E. Krieger Publishing, 1979.

FRANK VAN DER LINDEN, *Lincoln: The Road to War*. Golden, CO: Fulcrum Publishing, 1998.

INDEX

Abraham Lincoln (Charnwood), 64
African Americans
  franchise for, 171–72
  had no voice in Southern
    secession, 75
  Lincoln's personal view of, 136–37
  numbers of, in Union troops, 113
  opinion on social equality for, 23
  overseas colonization of, 114,
    150–51
Ainsworth, F.C., 106
American Civil War, The (Parish),
  148
Anderson, Robert, 19, 44, 53
And the War Came (Stampp), 35
Antietam, battle of, 78
Argyll, duke of, 65
Arnold, Isaac N., 180, 188
Articles of Confederation and
  Perpetual Union, 64
Ashley, James M., 157, 180, 187

Baldwin, John B., 47
Bangor Democrat (newspaper), 46
Banks, Nathaniel P., 170
Bates, Edward, 41, 42, 90
  and habeas corpus suspension, 87,
    93
Bell, John, 37, 41
Binney, Horace, 90, 93, 95
Blair, Francis P., 160, 161
Blair, Montgomery, 42, 160
Booth, John Wilkes, 27–28
Breckinridge, John, 37, 41
Bright, John, 170, 172
Brown, B. Gratz, 161, 164
Browning, Orville, 60
Brownson, Orestes C., 116
Buchanan, James, 58, 65

Bull Run, second battle of, 78
Burnside, Ambrose E., 117
Burr, Aaron, 95
Butler, Benjamin F., 163

Calhoun, John C., 70
Cameron, Simon, 54
Campbell, John A., 19, 45, 174, 175
Cartwright, Peter, 14
Chancellorsville, battle of, 78
Charnwood, Lord, 63
Chase, Salmon P., 59, 117, 155
  on seceded states, 157
Chew, Robert S., 47
Chicago Times (newspaper), 25
Chichamauga, battle of, 78
Civil War
  could have been avoided, 49–50
  death toll of, 29
  first shot of, 19–20, 48–49
  justifications for
    abolition of slavery, 77–80
    preservation of Union, 63–72,
      74–77, 151
  Lincoln's handling of political
    battle leading to, 39–50
  Lincoln used Fort Sumter to
    provoke South into, 51–56
    con, 57–62
Colfax, Schuyler, 187
Compromise of 1850, 33, 34
Confederate States of America
  blockade of ports in, 85–86
  formation of, 17
  map of, 23
Confiscation Acts of 1862, 24, 119,
  121–23, 133, 152
  debate over, 124–25
Constitution, U.S., 10

amendability of, 182
amendments
  Twelfth, 181
  Thirteenth, 26, 80, 171
    Democratic opposition to,
      180–83
    Lincoln was responsible for
      passage of, 178–89
  Declaration of Independence as
    essential part of, 140
  and reconstruction plan of
    radicals, 155
  and suspension of habeas corpus,
    93, 97
Cooke, Henry, 125
Cox, LaWanda, 129
Cox, Samuel S., 116
Craven, Avery, 146
Crawford, Samuel Wylie, 43
Crittenden, John, 32
Crittenden Compromise, 127–28
  Lincoln should have supported,
    32–38
Current, Richard N., 57, 178
Curtis, Samuel R., 161

Davis, Henry Winter, 176
Davis, Jefferson, 17, 19, 27–28, 64,
  173
  and Fort Sumter crisis, 52–53
Declaration of Independence, 10,
  139
  as essential part of Constitution,
    140
  Lincoln on, 72
Douglas, Stephen A., 14, 15, 37, 41
  see also Lincoln-Douglas debates
Douglass, Frederick, 136
  on the Emancipation
    Proclamation, 118
Drake, Charles D., 161, 162
Dred Scott decision, 15, 143
Dunning, William Archibald, 84

Emancipation Proclamation, 22, 24

effects of, 25, 115
Lincoln's restraint in wording of,
  134–36
as political expedient, 77
radical Republicans forced Lincoln
  to adopt, 119–28
as a war measure, 112–14
Emancipation Proclamation, The
  (Franklin), 111–18
Essays on the Civil War and
  Reconstruction (Dunning), 84
Ex parte Milligan, 102

Federalist Papers, 140
Fessenden, William Pitt, 122, 125
"fire-eaters," 16, 41
Fish, Hamilton, 122
Fort Sumter crisis, 18–20, 42–44
  Lincoln used to provoke South
    into war, 51–56
  con, 57–62
Fourteen Points, 81
Fowler, William C., 116
Fox, Gustavus V., 19, 42–43, 46, 56
Franklin, John Hope, 111
Fredericksburg, battle of, 78
Fredrickson, George, 136, 137
Freedmen's Bureau, 165
Freedom Under Lincoln (Sprague),
  98
Frémont, John C., 24, 133
  and reconstruction in Missouri,
    160
Fugitive Slave Law, 33

Gamble, Hamilton, 160–63
Garrison, William Lloyd, 80, 189
  on the Emancipation
    Proclamation, 118
Gettysburg, battle of, 78
Gettysburg Address, 10
Grant, Ulysses S., 27, 97, 173
Greeley, Horace, 22, 112, 122, 134
Gurowski, Count, 166
Gwin, William M., 101

habeas corpus, 94
 suspension of, 21–22, 86–89
  arrests under, 106, 108
  Chief Justice Taney on, 87
  constitutionality of, 93
  to increasingly large areas, 101
  as presidential function, 96–97
  was aimed at draft resistance,
   105
  was justified, 90–98
Hahn, Michael, 148, 165
Hallam, Henry, 53
Hamilton, Alexander, 140
Hamilton, James, 156
Hamlin, Hannibal, 188
Harney, William S., 160
Hay, John, 62, 91, 164, 179
Henderson, John B., 164, 179
Hesseltine, William B., 167
Hill, Adams S., 123
Hofstadter, Richard, 78
House Divided speech, 15
Howard, Jacob, 124
Hunter, David, 24
Hurlbut, Stephen A., 59, 165
Hyman, Harold M., 131

Illinois *State Journal* (newspaper), 25
Inaugural Address
 first, 16
  and secession crisis, 17, 41–42
 second, 80–81

Jacobins. *See* Republicans, radical
Jaffa, Harry, 144
Jay, John, 140
Jefferson, Thomas, 67, 142
 and right of revolution, 76
Johnson, Andrew, 158
 reconstruction under, 149, 176
Johnston, Joseph E., 173
Johnston, Sarah Bush, 12
Julian, George W., 150, 186

Kansas-Nebraska Act of 1854, 14–15

Kelly, Alfred H., 131
Kentucky, 100

Lamon, Ward Hill, 43, 45
Lansing, Robert, 82
Lee, Robert E., 20, 165
Lincoln, Abraham
 address to special session of
  Congress, 68–69
 assassination of, 28
 birth of, 11
 burden of war on, 78–79
 and colonization of freed slaves,
  114, 150–51
 conflict over Fort Sumter, 44–45
 early political life of, 12–14
 1860 election of, 16, 37, 41
  endangered slavery's future,
   67–70
 ending of slavery and preservation
  of the Union were inseparable
  goals of, 138–44
 and justifications for Civil War
  abolition of slavery, 77–80
  to preserve Union, 63–72, 76–77,
   151
 legacy of, 28–30
 letter to Fox, 56
 marriage to Mary Todd, 14
 message to Thirty-Eighth
  Congress, 184–85
 patriotism of, 71–72
 on radical Republicans, 164
 on Reconstruction
  in Louisiana, 165–66
  in Missouri, 161–62, 163, 164
 Reconstruction plan of, 150–53,
  173–75
  became increasingly radical,
   154–66
  collapse of, 175–76
  myth of, 177
 on right of revolution, 77
 statesmanship of, 139–40
 on states' rights, 156

suspension of civil liberties by
  has been exaggerated, 104–10
  was reluctant, 98–103
used Fort Sumter crisis to provoke
  South into war, 51–56
  con, 57–62
views of
  on blacks, 136–37
  on slavery, 12, 15, 140–41, 142,
  186
Lincoln, Nancy, 11, 12
Lincoln, Thomas, 11
Lincoln, the President (Randall and
  Current), 178
Lincoln and Black Freedom (Cox),
  129
*Lincoln and His Party in the
  Secession Crisis* (Potter), 32
Lincoln and the First Shot (Current),
  57
Lincoln and the Radicals (Williams),
  119
Lincoln-Douglas debates, 16, 130,
  141–42
Lincoln's Plan of Reconstruction
  (Hesseltine), 167
Lincoln Takes Command (Tilley), 51
Livingstone, David, 138
Lothrop, Thornton K., 54
Louisiana
  10 percent plan in, 147–48
Lunt, George, 54

Madison, James, 140
Martin v. Mott, 95
Maryland, 100
McClellan, George B., 20–21, 121,
  183
McPherson, James M., 104, 139
Missouri, 100
  Reconstruction in, 160–62
Missouri Compromise of 1820, 14,
  34, 142, 143
Morgan, E.D., 183
Morris, Gouverneur, 95

Morse, John T., 54

National Intelligencer, 163
nationalism
  vs. secession, 75–76
Neely, Mark E., Jr., 107, 139
New York Evening Day-Book, 46
New York *Herald* (newspaper), 43,
  54
New York Times (newspaper), 171
New York *Tribune* (newspaper), 122
New York World (newspaper), 158
Nicolay, John, 55, 62, 91, 179
Northwest Ordinance of 1787, 180

Odell, Moses F., 186
*Ordeal by Fire: The Civil War and
  Reconstruction* (McPherson), 104

Parish, Peter J., 148
Parker, Theodore, 155
Philadelphia *Press* (newspaper), 76
Phillips, Wendell, 117, 155
Pickens, Francis W., 19, 20, 43, 61
Pickney, Charles, 94
Pierpont, Francis Harrison, 149, 170
Pike, Frederick A., 120
Pope, John, 120, 127
Porter, David, 173
Potter, David M., 32
Powell, Lewis Thorton, 28
"Prayer of Twenty Millions"
  (Greeley), 112
prisons, 21–22, 89
Prize Cases, 86
Pruyn, John, 181

Quantrill, William, 162

Radical Republicans, The
  (Trefousse), 154
Ramsdell, Charles W., 59
Randall, J.G., 61, 90, 131, 178
Reconstruction, 146
  in border states, 159–60

as executive vs. legislative
function, 169–70
under Johnson, 149, 155, 176
Lincoln's plan for, 150–53
became increasingly radical,
154–66
myth behind, 177
in Louisiana, 147–48, 165–66
in Missouri, 160–62
*Reconstruction: The Ending of the
Civil War* (Craven), 146
Republicans, radical, 16
and black suffrage, 171–72
forced Lincoln to adopt
emancipation, 119–28
con, 129–37
Lincoln's move toward, 162–65
reconstruction plan of, 155–57
R.H. Shannon (ship), 58
Robinson, Charles D., 151
Rollins, James S., 185–86

Schlesinger, Arthur, Jr., 82
Schofield, John M., 162
Scott, Dred, 15
Scott, Winfield, 42, 54, 87
secession
crisis over, 17–18
Lincoln's view of, 81, 168–69
vs. nationalism, 75–76
question over legality of, 64–65
responsibility for, 70
slavery as grounds for, 65–67,
138–44
Southern threats of, 16
self-determination, doctrine of, 74,
75
Lincoln's legacy on, 81
Seven Days' battles, 78
Seward, William H., 28, 45, 105,
122, 126
Sherman, William T., 173
Shiloh, battle of, 78
slavery
conflict between, in Constitution

vs. Declaration of Independence,
10–11
ending of, and preservation of the
Union, were inseparable goals to
Lincoln, 138–44
as grounds for secession, 65–67
Lincoln's views on, 12, 15, 140–41,
142, 186
Speed, James, 166, 174
Sprague, Dean, 98
Stampp, Kenneth M., 35, 73
Stanton, Edwin M., 105, 106, 153
"State Suicide" doctrine, 156, 158
Stephens, Alexander, 67
on slavery as cause of secession, 76
Stevens, Thaddeus, 116, 117, 124,
168, 187
Stowe, Harriet Beecher, 29
Stuart, John Todd, 13
Sumner, Charles, 116, 121, 148, 156,
177
and antislavery amendment, 179
and "State Suicide" doctrine,
157–58, 168
Supreme Court
and Dred Scott decision, 15, 143
on presidential right to establish
blockade, 85–86
on suspension of habeas corpus,
102–103

Taney, Roger B., 15
and suspension of habeas corpus,
87, 88, 91
10 percent plan, 27
failure of, 146–53
Thirteenth Amendment. *See*
Constitution, U.S.
Tilley, John Shipley, 51
Todd, Mary, 14
Totten, Joseph Gilbert, 54
Trefousse, Hans L., 154
Trumbull, Lyman, 123, 148, 171, 179

Union, preservation of

and ending of slavery, 138–44
as justification for Civil War,
   63–72, 74–77, 151
political events ensuring, 99–100

Vallandigham, Clement L., 21, 103,
   116
arrest of, 101–102
Vance, Z.B., 173
van der Linden, Frank, 39
Virginia
   decommissioning of Rebel troops
      in, 174–75

Wade, Benjamin, 124, 125, 157, 171
Wade-Davis Bill, 146, 147
Wadsworth, James S., 123
Wall, James W., 101
War of 1812, 75
Weitzel, Godfrey, 174, 175
Welles, Gideon, 59, 126, 174
Whig Party
   Lincoln as candidate for, 14
Whiskey Rebellion (1794), 85, 95
Williams, T. Harry, 119
Wilson, Henry, 116, 124
Wilson, Woodrow, 81